NORTH AMERICAN RAILROADS TODAY

Geoffrey Freeman Allen

Brian Trodd Publishing House Limited

Published in 1990 by
Brian Trodd Publishing House Limited
27 Swinton Street, London WC1X 9NW

ISBN 1 85361 068 2

Printed in Spain

Typeset in England
by Area Graphics Ltd

Page 1: Amtrak's Broadway Limited, en route from New York and Washington to Chicago, rounds Pennsylvania's Horseshoe Curve which cuts through the Appalachians.

Title page: A solid grain train of the Chessie System at Fostoria, Ohio.

Right: One of Amtrak's AEM-7 electric locomotives leans to a curve in the New York-Washington Northeast Corridor with a high-speed Metroliner.

Following pages: A quartet of GM-EMD SD40-2 locomotives blasts out of Cheyenne, Wyoming, with a 59-car TOFC train.

NORTH AMERICAN RAILROADS TODAY

Contents

INTRODUCTION

North American railroading today is the invigorating story of a great industry's resurgence, weathering a recent recession deep enough to have brought about a wave of major system bankruptcies had it hit ten years ago.

So far as the major US railroads are concerned, it is a tale of steady technical and operating improvements, exploiting every possible application of the hectic advance in electronics technology. Control of traffic and equipment has been tightened by computer-based data transmission systems, by computerized aid for dispatchers, automated sorting of trains in classification yards, and a wide range of ancillary equipment, such as electronic devices employing voice synthesizers which radio to engineers or control centers precise, spoken warnings of overheated axleboxes they have detected in passing trains. The latest diesel locomotives are not only a substantial degree more energy-efficient than those of only a decade ago, but they also maximize the potential of electronics to improve performance and simplify maintenance in thoroughly efficient order. They have much better track to travel on, thanks to the millions of dollars recently invested in sophisticated, labor-saving machines to perform every kind of track maintenance, and plowed in to a sustained high level of track renewal.

Helped by Washington's dismantling

6

of historic curbs on their commercial freedom, US railroads are not only developing impressive new hauls in their staple bulk commodity traffics like coal, but breaking more strongly by the year into the general merchandise market. This is with the piggybacking of road trailers and containers, a business in which the railroads are gaining new efficiency, on the one hand by acquiring new marketing expertise to exploit their commercial freedom, on the other by new cost-saving practices and hardware.

The Canadian scene is just as exciting. With Japanese demand for minerals seemingly inexhaustible, both major Canadian railroads are spending huge sums to enlarge their transcontinental capacity and in British Columbia a railroad has been electrified to move vast tonnages of Japan-bound coal.

Neither in the US nor in Canada is the passenger train dead, least of all in the big cities, where new building of rapid transit lines is at one of the highest levels in the world. The intriguing question, though, is which pair of those cities will be first to enjoy a connecting high-speed rail service on a par with Europe's fastest or Japan's Shinkansen. As we enter the 1990s, such an American enterprise approaches reality.

1
THE NEW FACE OF US RAILROADING

If it had hit ten years earlier, an economic recession of the severity experienced in the early 1980s would have had Wall Street analysts forecasting a fresh wave of bankruptcies which ravaged US railroads in the late 1960s. In 1980-82 the industrial downturn knocked away more than 13 percent of the gross ton-mileage registered by the 30 freight-hauling Class I US railroads, which in the Association of American Railroads (AAR) classification ruling since the start of 1978 are those pulling in over $50 million operating revenue a year (the purely passenger-operating Amtrak also meets this qualification). However though one or two Class I systems slid into the red, it was no more than a temporary inconvenience. Still more of a contrast to valuation of railroad prospects a decade earlier was the view of a good many market seers, not only that the railroads would revive in step with the national economy, but that in many cases their stocks were a sound growth buy.

One reason for this confidence was the much healthier financial state of the railroad industry as it faced the 1980s slump. Adjusted to constant dollar values, the combined net revenue of the Class I railroads in 1981 was more than three times their income at the start of the 1970s. Even in the two dire years that followed, 1982-83, they posted a total net well up on their results in the early 1970s.

Plenty more statistics testified to the railroads' steadily advancing technical and commercial efficiency, but just one comparison must suffice here. In 1971 the Class I railroads together logged 740 billion freight ton-miles, but were then employing over 544,300 men. In 1980 the figures were 919 billion ton-miles, with staff down to just under 459,000. By 1983 the recession had cut ton-mileage to 825,000, but the total of Class I system employees had dropped much more steeply, to a little below 335,300. That represented an 80 percent improvement in the productive use of labor in a dozen years. (In 1949, incidentally, Class I railroad employees numbered over 1.19 million!)

Federal action takes some of the credit for the upturn in US railroad fortunes. It became inescapable when, in the fading 1960s, the US passenger train was heading for extinction (how that was forestalled is discussed elsewhere); and, far graver, railroading generally throughout the Northeast faced total collapse as economic trends peculiar to that region aggravated problems that were common to the whole railroad industry.

By the 1960s the railroads' financial performance had deteriorated to the extent that the average return on the Class I systems' capital was less than 3 percent. Neither Washington nor railroad managements had responded positively to the impact of post-war trucking's upsurge on traditional rail transportation patterns and method. Spurred by the spread of new highways, by cheap fuel, and by vehicle development, it had robbed the railroads of a huge tonnage of lucrative general merchandise traffic and left them increasingly dependent on lower-rated bulk mineral and commodity freight.

Reaction to the rapid expansion of domestic air services, to keener intercity bus competition from Greyhound and others, and to wider-ranging use of the private automobile was more lively.

Right: In the fading years of pre-Amtrak long-haul passenger service, the Pennsylvania's 18-car "Congressional" is fronted by one of the classic GG-1 electrics.

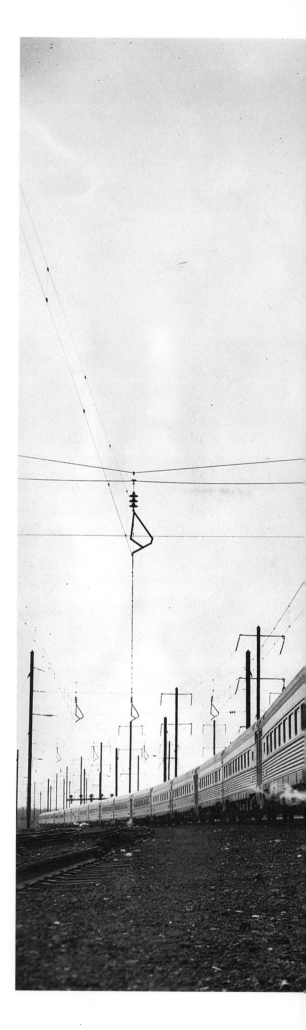

Left: Maintenance and repair of the track is nowadays fully mechanized.

But it was not swift enough to stem industry-wide losses averaging almost $650 million a year in the second half of the 1950s, despite the thousands of passenger-route miles that were already being abandoned and which by 1967 had more than halved the percentage of the national rail network carrying passenger trains. Some railroads were already out of the passenger business altogether.

To be fair, the pace of withdrawal from financially debilitating passenger service was to an extent dictated by the need to seek Interstate Commerce Commission (ICC) approval for each and every abandonment. This was just one of the shackles inherited from the late 19th-century legislation enacted to prevent railroads abusing their monopoly on economic bulk transportation, whether of passengers or freight. Much more crippling, though, were the archaic statutes which still strictly limited railroads' freedom of commercial maneuver – and which consequently stifled managerial initiative in face of drastically changed freight market conditions. Sparkling new railroad managerial talent became progressively harder to recruit as the 1960s progressed, in fact.

The railroad labor unions, one ought

to add, saw nothing in the railroads' deepening financial crisis to justify a relaxation of their historic work-rules. Moreover, the courageous Florida East Coast refused in the early 1960s to be enslaved by the rigidity of 100-mile train-crew working days or a five-man train-crew requirement, and withdrew from the national railroad labor negotiations and deals that accepted such conditions. It had to withstand not only a year of strikes and sabotage, but also heavy pressure from the Kennedy Administration to settle on the labor unions' terms, before it established its right to attack its long-running deficit on its own terms.

Contraction of investment resources was the obvious consequence of the railroads' dwindling income. Track maintenance was the principal casualty. On the more financially unsound systems the gap between track repair or renewal need and achievement was widening by the year. This meant that speed restrictions over bad-order sections were proliferating, extending transits, and injecting new unreliabilities into the quality of service, to make even more forlorn the battle with truckers for the well-paying categories of freight.

Several major railroads had sought

greater financial strength through merger since World War II, either to rationalize parallel, competing systems or to stitch systems together end-to-end for longer through-haul opportunities. At the start of 1959, for instance, the Virginian had been absorbed by Norfolk & Western, merging two of the chief coal hauliers from the eastern mines to the east coast shipment ports. Four years later Chesapeake & Ohio had taken control of neighboring Baltimore & Ohio and the Central of Georgia had passed into Southern Railway hands. The most amazing marriage was that first announced in 1957, to the astonishment of the rest of the industry: the alliance of the giant arch-rivals of the East, the Pennsylvania and New York Central. Both were desperately in need of economies, chiefly because of horrendous losses on passenger operation – $54.7 million in Pennsy's case, $48.5 million in NYC's in 1956; in 1957 NYC's net revenue was slashed by two-thirds, Pennsy's by almost half, and neither on its own looked capable of plugging the drain.

However the merger of the two systems as Penn-Central was not effected until 1968. Every claim of disadvantage from the merger had to be heard and dissected by the ICC; and at that time there was no statutory obligation on the ICC to pronounce on the case within a reasonable time-scale. The ICC's leisurely deliberation was not the end of the rigmarole either, as appellants dissatisfied with their findings could always seek to get ICC judgments overruled in the courts: the last hurdle cleared by the Penn-Central merger was, in fact, the US Supreme Court. Even so, Penn-Central was not a record in protracted consideration of a merger case. In the 1960s and early 1970s the ICC took 12 years, no less, to summon up an endorsement of Rock Island's application to merge with Union Pacific. By then Union Pacific had lost interest and the Rock was left to slip

Right: A popular over-the-road workhorse of the early 1980s: a brace of GM SD40-2s wheel a Burlington Northern freight.

back into bankruptcy, which eventually destroyed it as an independent system in the early 1980s.

By the time the Penn-Central merger was finally approved, an archangelic management team would have had its work cut out to stave off financial catastrophe. Its railroad operations were losing around $150 million a year, chiefly because PC was running almost three-quarters of the US surviving inter-city passenger trains; they were responsible for almost half the deficit purely on their avoidable costs – that is, the obvious direct expenses of running the trains, with no account taken of their share of track, signaling, and other fixed railroad costs. Neither constituent company had managed better than 0.6 percent return on capital employed since 1961. The ICC then compounded their financial troubles by insisting that the merged system embrace the hopelessly sick New Haven system, north of New York. Worse yet, the Pennsy had been borrowing heavily to follow Union Pacific and others into diversification, especially into property development countrywide. With the country's economy regressing at the close of the 1960s, that was yielding a return well below expectations. Add to all this the onset of cost inflation, and the outlook was in any event grim.

It was hopeless when, from board to ground level, age-old Pennsy-NYC jealousies and dogmatic differences were immediately allowed not merely to surface but to permeate every reorganization and rationalization project. None of the financial economies forecast from the merger were realized; managers from the two former systems who were now thrown together often refused to collaborate; and dogfights aggravated an operational confusion arising from the incompatibility of the two railroads' data transmission systems, which had freight customers decamping to the highways in droves.

In the background, sagging US industrial output and labor strikes were accelerating the drain on PC resources – so much so that in the first quarter of 1970 PC losses were already soaring beyond the system's full 1969 deficit. In May that year, Wall Street sensed irreversible descent to disaster and refused any more loans. A desperate PC sought help from Washington, which had just bailed out another industrial giant, aircraft manufacturer Lockheed, but was rebuffed by Congress. The only course left was to file a bankruptcy petition. It was the largest-scale collapse of an industry in US history.

The fall of PC had a domino effect on its smaller northeastern neighbors, all of which had been teetering on the brink of insolvency. One of the external factors contributing to PC's downfall was the downward trend of the Northeast's heavy industrial traffic, the result partly of a move out of coal and into oil or gas as a fuel, partly of the depression in the steel and auto industries, and partly of the drift of smokestack industry out of the region. So the 1970 bankruptcy of the 1,100-mile Lehigh Valley was unsurprising; that railroad had been built essentially to transport anthracite coal. The 3,189-mile Erie-Lackawanna went the same

way in 1972. Others to tumble in the late 1960s and early 1970s were the Central of New Jersey, the Reading, the Lehigh & Hudson River, and the Ann Arbor (though the Reading Company, like PC, is among former railroad concerns still involved in the activities into which it diversified).

In the wake of PC's bankruptcy, the trustees appointed to attempt a reorganization of the corporation's railroad business (under a section of US law specifically allowing US railroads a tax-free and debt-free moratorium to essay a financial turnround) struggled to rationalize the system's gross excess of duplicate routes and terminals; to trim its labor costs; to counter the loss of heavy industrial freight by developing a competitive intermodal system for high-rated merchandise; and to offload heavily loss-making commuter passenger operations in Boston, New York, and Philadelphia on to the relevant state administrations. Success was scant. All the time the railroad assets were sinking further into disrepair and decrepitude.

Washington had to intervene. The first step was the Regional Rail Reorganization Act of 1973 – since known as the "3-R" – which set up the United States Railway Administration (USRA)

to contrive a viable scheme for a rationalized rail system in the Northeast.
That was followed in 1976 by the Rail
Revitalization & Reform Act – the "4-R"
–which, under USRA's supervision, set
up the Consolidated Rail Corporation,
or Conrail, to run a conglomeration of
PC and the six other railroads which it
had helped to suck into bankruptcy.

The 4-R Act also tackled the inability
of railroads to generate adequate funds
for essential plant upkeep by creating a
$1.6 billion fund with which the Federal
Railroad Administration (FRA) – a
component of the Department of Transportation (DOT) – could underwrite and
get moving the overdue infrastructure
rehabilitation of many busy routes
interlining major markets. This money,
incidentally, was additional to the considerable funds established to launch
Conrail and the new national intercity
passenger train operator, Amtrak.

The 4-R Act further clamped a 2½-
year time limit on the ICC's consideration of merger applications. That re-
flected not only a chastened Washington's embarrassment at its failure to
foresee and forestall disaster in the
Northeast, but also its arousal to the
irrelevance of so many historic anti-
pathies to mega-railroad proposals.
This was apparent with the patent
benefits quickly realized from the
March 1970 forging of the country's
longest system, the 26,500-mile Burlington Northern (BN) after years of
hearings which, as in the Penn-Central
case, reached their climax in the US
Supreme Court.

Amalgamation of railroads partici-
pating in or competing for traffic between the Great Lakes and the West
Coast had been attempted more than
once, starting with the effort of railroad
empire-builder James J Hill in 1893.
All had been blocked by variations on
the theme of antitrust paranoia. Ultimate achievement in BN was no shot-
gun marriage in the face of financial
difficulty, but a voluntary alliance of
four companies which recognized the
overwhelming advantages of concentrating their transcontinental freight

on the easiest of two parallel routes
through the Cascade Mountains, for example; and of through diesel locomotives and trains running from West
Coast ports to Chicago, instead of the
much less productive operation involved in traction changes and train reclassification at each others' frontiers.

The four original constituents of BN
were the Great Northern, Northern
Pacific, the Chicago, Burlington &
Quincy, and the Spokane, Portland &
Seattle. In 1980 BN also gathered in the

St Louis-San Francisco, best-known as
the 'Frisco,' followed in 1981 by the
Colorado & Southern, a former CB & Q
subsidiary, and at the start of 1983 by
the Fort Worth & Denver.

Today BN is a network of over 29,200
route-miles, operating in 25 US states
and two Canadian provinces, and
stretching from Washington and Ore-
gon in the west to Minneapolis-St Paul,
Chicago, and St Louis and as far south
as Houston, Texas, and Pensacola, Florida. Almost two-thirds of its gross re-

Left: A Portec machine clips rail to new concrete sleepers.

Below left: Track inspection at 80mph in Conrail's $2 million track geometry car: TV screen above window displays close-up of track from five underfloor cameras.

Below: An Illinois Central Gulf unit coal train heads for Chicago from southern Illinois mines, with GM-EMD GP-11 diesels in charge.

venue derives from movement of three commodities: coal, grain, and forest products. In two of these departments, coal and grain, it is a national leader in tonnage hauled annually: indeed, as a grain mover it has no equal.

Like a number of other major railroads, BN is part of a conglomerate. As the earlier postwar years stripped the financial gloss from railroading, several companies looked to offset the worsening performance of their prime business by diversifying – the hapless Pennsylvania's move into property development has already been mentioned. Elsewhere, the Atchison, Topeka & Santa Fe (ATSF) or Santa Fe, became in 1968 the subsidiary of Santa Fe Industries, whose interests today embrace other transportation modes, natural resources, real estate, construction, and forest products. Southern Pacific (SP) is a member of the Southern Pacific Transportation Co, with very extensive land ownings, timberland, and mineral rights in its portfolio as well as pipeline operations. To cite just one more example, Union Pacific Corporation, the parent of the Union Pacific Railroad (UP), own major petroleum/ petro-chemical and mining companies as well as an industrial development enterprise. As for BN, the activities of Burlington Northern Inc, of which it is a subsidiary, run the gamut from forestry products to oil and gas exploration and ore mining.

The striking feature of this diversification is that to date only two major companies have found other industrial activities profitable enough that they would be better out of their founding business, railroading. In the 1950s the dynamic Ben Heinemann fought to weld together some of the financially sick railroads in the Midwest into an integral, viable system. By 1966 he had achieved a Chicago & North Western (C&NW) that turned in a resounding operational surplus of some $26 million. However further Heinemann schemes to enlarge the C&NW railroad empire, notably the acquisition of the Rock Island and Milwaukee Roads to estab-

lish virtually a single network for the region, were frustrated.

Its momentum checked, C&NW slid back into the red. Back in 1965 Heinemann had formed Northwest Industries to diversify into non-rail business; this proved tremendously profitable and by the end of the decade Northwest Industries was eager to be rid of C&NW. A disenchanted Heinemann, so recently the eagerest beaver on the US rail scene industry, now owned that he had become "totally discontented with the railroad industry . . . its rate of return is disgustingly inadequate." In 1972 the sale of C&NW and certain of its subsidiaries to the railroad's employees was completed and in that guise the railroad functions today under the title of Chicago & North Western Transportation Co.

Disposal of another Class I system, the Illinois Central Gulf (ICG), created through the 1972 merger of Illinois Central and Gulf, Mobile & Ohio encompassing a 9,660 route-mile system stretching from Chicago, Omaha, and Sioux City southward to Montgomery, Mobile, and New Orleans, was still only an intention in early 1984. Illinois Central had a diversification frontrunner, forming IC Industries as early as 1962, and this conglomerate became ICG's parent. Since the 1972 merger that established ICG the parent has already presided over a 28 percent truncation of route-mileage, but it has been aiming for an ultimate core system of little more than 5,000 route-miles, to fine down to the highest-volume routes on its books. A further 700 route-miles, along with 30 locomotives and 1,500 freight cars, were being sold in eastern Mississippi and neighboring states in the course of 1984, for operation by Kyle Railways of San Diego under L B Foster & Co (Pittsburgh) ownership. Nevertheless, IC Industries, now big in the food and drink business and with other interests in automotive and machinery component manufacture, and in defense items, pronounced sale of ICG to be a priority objective as soon as an acceptable buyer materialized.

Although the economic disruption engaged the railroads in the mid-1970s, driving the average return on Class I system investment to an abysmal 1.24 percent in 1977, none of the other big railroads were denied investment by their parent corporations. BN, for instance, has been allowed since 1976 to plow over $1,500 million into infrastructure improvements and more than $600 million into new traction and cars to enlarge its coal-carrying capacity in face of the rising demand for export coal, also of increased domestic consumption as industry shied away from high-priced oil fuel, and clean-air legislation put a premium on low sulphur coal mined in BN's Wyoming and Montana territory. On the other hand the depressed financial state of railroading in the mid-1970s, together with the clear testimony that the technical means to recoup some of the lost intercity merchandise freight had been perfected, swelled railroad executive clamor for release from the chains of ICC regulatory law. In its essentials this was encompassed in the hallowed provision of the Interstate Commerce Act of 1887.

The Kennedy Administration had professed its intention to attack the problem, but deregulation of transport did not get underway until Carter's presidency. First to be thrown to the free play of market forces, in October 1979, was air transport. Deregulation unleashed an internecine fare-cutting war on plum routes and spawned a rash of small airlines to take over the less remunerative routes abandoned by the majors. Next followed the deregulation of the trucking industry: but no more than 40 percent of motor-carrier tonnage had been subject to ICC regulation anyway.

Meanwhile the railroads stayed almost completely regulated. Apart from recent exemption in respect of fresh fruit and vegetable traffic, they were still hog-tied by the same restrictions on their rate-making and freedom to contract for long-term business – or contract out of loss-making routes and services – as applied before more than 40,000 miles of Interstate Highway were laid across the country, and at the price of over 100 billion taxpayers' dollars which trucker users were in no way fully contributing toward. The railroads were not only financially responsible for the full maintenance of their right-of-way, but obliged to pay local taxes on it.

The airline and trucking industries had fought fiercely to abort their deregulation, principally for fear of its opening up the business to new entrants who would dilute the profits of established concerns. That was obviously not a risk in the railroad industry. Nevertheless, rail chiefs were not unanimous in pressing for deregulation. For example, Norfolk & Western's (NW) then President, John P Fishwick, argued in 1979 that it should wait until the potential inter-railroad competition had been diminished by further mergers. He knew his industry. When deregulation was enacted, the retrograde response of some railroads was to go for their neighbors' traffic with riskily low-priced offers, and not develop a marketing expertise to broach markets that had been previously inaccessible. But then, not one railroad executive of 1979 had ever been born when a US railroad last had any need to learn how to turn a marketplace deal on price.

After a tortured Congressional passage, during which it barely escaped derailment by determined coal-mining and coal-burning public utility interests convinced that deregulation would make them captive to rail transportation rate exploitation, President Carter signed the necessary legislation in October 1980. It is known as the Staggers Act, in honor of sponsoring Representative Harley O Staggers, a Democrat of West Virginia.

In brief, the Staggers Act allowed market forces much more play in setting railroad freight rates. The rigid enforcement of ICC maximum and minimum rates was over. Too often in the past the ICC had set a ceiling on rates with far more solicitude for power-

ful shippers or the clout of a geographical area than for the railroads' desperate need of a fair return to finance the upkeep of their tracks and rolling stock, and never mind their stockholders. The poor state of a good deal of track and vehicles was an inevitable result. The Staggers Act enshrined the importance of allowing railroads a fair margin above the direct costs of moving traffic, and set a floor for that margin: if a railroad's return fell below it, then the railroad could hike its rate back on the right side without reference to the ICC.

Staggers further authorized the ICC to exempt entirely any traffic and services it deemed needless of regulation; only when railroads exercised "market dominance" was much control still thought reasonable. The most important traffics completely deregulated up to the end of 1984 were perishables, intermodel traffic (this release was accompanied by license for railroads to run their own complementary trucking – nationwide if they wished to apply for such authority – so as to offer total door-to-door transportation), and export coal.

Another widely welcomed provision of Staggers was freedom for railroads to negotiate individual price and service contracts with their customers, regardless of terms offered by other systems or carriers, or of any rates already offered for comparable traffic. Less universally applauded was abolition of the "joint rate" principle, whereby the same tariff had previously to be charged over all competing rail routes between two points, no matter what their disparity in distance (any alteration of that rate was debarred unless each railroad concerned consented to the change, moreover).

An end to joint rate-setting naturally benefited many shippers, who could play the field to get a better rate. It squeezed railroads untouched by the mega-mergers of the 1980s, as the new giant systems moved to keep traffic on their own tracks for the maximum mileage of each transit. Missouri-Kansas-Texas (the "Katy"), for instance, has had to battle with pinched rates to

keep from the clutches of Burlington Northern and the Union Pacific-Missouri Pacific alliance its shipment freight between its Kansas City and St Louis gateways and the Gulf ports.

Some Jeremiahs forecast that the compression of railroads into a few giant networks which deregulation would encourage, would simply create mammoths content to turn an easy profit by persistent price-raising on convenient traffics like coal. In time that would build up such customer resistance that the only option left would be the unthinkable, railroad nationalization.

Certainly the railroads' exploitation of deregulation has begun to worry the competition. By 1984 efforts to restore at least a measure of regulation were being mounted, one sponsored by the barge operators. The export coal industry's persistent litigation over its new rates had achieved the success of a Washington Appeal Court judgment that the ICC's deregulation of its traffic was an "improper" interpretation of the Staggers Act's intent.

But most of the complaints were unwarranted. Statistics issued by the Association of American Railroads in early 1982 showed that since the Staggers Act's passage far more rates had been cut than raised. More significantly, there were already signs of the railroads grabbing a bigger share of some markets, and of lifting their net earnings. That was reinforcing the faith of the holding companies in their railroad subsidiaries, to the extent that these conglomerates were plowing between 64 and 78 percent of their total investment resources into their rail subsidiaries. A high proportion of those dollars was being wisely invested in track upgrading of routes carrying traffic particularly sensitive to quality of service.

Belief that deregulation would be followed by new grouping moves in the railroad industry was not unjustified, however. Before 1980 was out, three massive new mergers were before the ICC.

2
THE AGE OF THE US MEGA-RAILROAD

In November 1980 the ICC pronounced its blessing on the molding of a new mega-railroad boasting even more route-miles than Burlington Northern at the latter's birth. What had once been 16 separate railroads, with an aggregate of 28,212 miles, were assembled under the wing of a new CSX Corporation, though by the fall of 1980 these 16 systems had already sorted themselves into two large groups.

One was the Chessie System, incorporated in 1973. This had fused the Chesapeake & Ohio, Baltimore & Ohio, Western Maryland (which by 1963 was 43 percent B&O-owned), and the Chicago South Shore & South Bend, an electrified interurban system with an important commuter passenger role which the C&O had acquired in 1967. B&O and C&O retain separate operating organizations within the Chessie System – as, naturally, does the Chicago South Shore & South Bend – but Western Maryland lost its identity and became part of B&O in 1983.

The Chessie System as a whole is the major US railroad coal hauler. C&O's chief routes link the coalfields of southern West Virginia, eastern Kentucky, and southern Ohio with the eastern seaboard, above all the shipment port of Newport News, Virginia; to the north with Detroit; and in the west with Chicago, Cincinnati, and Louisville. Another key route connects Chicago with Detroit and Buffalo. B&O's principal main lines run from Philadelphia through Baltimore and Washington, DC to Cumberland, Maryland, and from there by separate routes to Chicago and St Louis. Another trunk reached from Cincinnati to Toledo, and B&O also penetrates the West Virginia coalfield.

The other constituent of the CSX Corporation was in 1980 the Seaboard Coast Line (SCL), though since the mid-1970s it had been promoting itself under the unofficial tag of the "Family Lines." This title coalesced a number of railroads, which had been assembled by a process of mergers spanning many years and too complex to recount here, and which blanketed the whole southeast of the country, from Chicago, Cincinnati, and Norfolk, Virginia, down to New Orleans, Tampa, and Miami, Florida. Chief components were the Atlantic Coast Line, Seaboard Air Line, Louisville & Nashville, Clinchfield, Georgia, and Atlanta & West Point Railroads, and the Western Railway of Alabama. The Louisville & Nashville was not formally merged with SCL until December 1982, whereupon the charter of SCL was rewritten under a new title, the Seaboard System Railroad.

Seaboard has both a crucial north-south transportation role and also important east-west routings throughout its territory. It reaches all the Atlantic coast ports from Richmond, Virginia, down to New Orleans on the Gulf, and also caters for several significant ports on the Mississippi and Ohio Rivers. Seaboard is, too, another of the coal-hauling majors, tapping reserves put at over 12,000 million tons in the Appalachian Mountains areas of Kentucky, Tennessee, southwest Virginia, and Alabama, and in the Midwestern states of Indiana and Illinois. Coal generates almost a quarter of Seaboard revenues, much of it fed to electric power utilities in the Southeast, Midwest, and along the Gulf coastline.

SCL had sought alliance with the neighboring Chessie System in 1978 to

Right: Four GM-EMD GP40-2 diesels lay down a blue exhaust haze, working hard on Conrail freight.

escape the clutches of Southern Pacific, owner of nearly 10 percent of SCL stock, which was bent on achieving the dream of a true transcontinental railroad. Marriage with another coal-hauling giant in the eastern half of the US made more immediate sense. At the time Chessie was flush with traction and coal hoppers, and with its own hopper-car manufacturing capacity, whereas the L&N member of the Seaboard family in particular was being harried by the ICC as well as its shippers for service short-comings traceable to inadequate equipment.

Within the CSX fold, the Chessie and Seaboard Systems retain not only their separate identities, but also their own management and control of operations. CSX also has a controlling interest in the Richmond, Fredericksburg & Potomac (RF&P), a system of much greater significance than its mere 113.8 miles of route might suggest. Fringing Conrail and the B&O at Washington, DC, and Seaboard at Richmond, Virginia, it is a vital bridge, particularly for intermodal traffic, and logs a volume of traffic worth $55 million in 1983. In that year RF&P's operating ratio – direct operating costs in relation to income – was a very robust 65.7 percent.

The reaction of the two other Class I systems confronting CSX with a giant,

Far left, top: More GP40-2s, this time in Chessie System service, powering a unit train of crushed rock near Daswell, Virginia.

Far left, below: Southern Pacific's busy intermodal traffic center at Los Angeles.

Left: A pair of Seaboard System's GM-EMD SD50 diesels ride a steel trestle with Appalachian coal, the railroad's biggest single traffic commodity.

Above right: Southern before merger: two SD45s and an SD40-2 have 147 freight cars in tow as they hammer over the grade crossing with the Chessie System at Charlottesville, Virginia.

Right: In pre-NS merger livery, a string of three GP-5s (one fronts the train), one GP30 and one GP18, all GM-EMD types, threads freight through Waynesboro, V.

unified railroad overlapping their territory was predictable. In April 1979 Norfolk & Western and Southern likewise opened merger talks. The courtship was chequered. For a period in 1979-80 talks foundered on a clash both of forward strategies and of powerful personalities, but once differences were resolved the ICC cleared the application to merge in only 15 months. In March 1982 it approved formation of Norfolk Southern Corporation (NS) as a holding company to coordinate the merger, which became fully effective at the start of the following June.

Norfolk & Western (NW), which in the 1950s and 1960s had accumulated several other roads by merger or lease, notably the Virginian, Nickel Plate, Pittsburgh & West Virginia, and Wabash, was the archetypal coal-hauling US railroad – and consequently the last to surrender steam traction to diesel. It still counts almost two-thirds of its total tonnage in coal. With a network stretching from the port (and NS base) of Norfolk, Virginia, westward to Kansas City and north to industrial Chicago, Detroit, and Cleveland, N&W digs deep into the rich coalfields of West Virginia, southern Ohio, and eastern Kentucky.

Southern also draws a considerable income from coal, though not so much as N&W; today coal accounts for about 40 percent of the combined NS railroads' revenue. Southern ranges over 13 states east of the Mississippi River, from St Louis, Cincinnati, Washington, DC, and Norfolk, Virginia, down to New Orleans and Jacksonville, Florida, tak-

ing in a chain of Atlantic coast ports from Norfolk southward. Consequently NS was essentially an end-to-end merger of the two railroads, which connect principally at East St Louis and Cincinnati, and at points in Virginia and North Carolina. In route-length, 17,860 miles at the time of merger, NS forged a network that trailed some way behind the extent of BN and CSX, but one that was and still is the most profitable in the whole Class I railroad industry: in 1983 its net income after taxes was $356.5 million on gross revenues of $3,148.1 million.

From the outset freight cars of the two NS systems were pooled, likewise workshop capacity, terminal, and yard installations, and rationalization of traction employment was followed by application of not particularly prepossessing corporate locomotive livery. But in general the two systems operate autonomously. An obvious benefit was the opening up of several efficient new single-system routes to and from the south-eastern US, in one case backed by the immediate construction of a new intermodal yard at Landers, Chicago.

The CSX and NS mergers, welding together as they did new single-system links between the south and not only the Midwest but also parts of the Northeast, naturally threatened erosion of Conrail traffic and raised fresh question marks against the prospects of that system. By the end of 1980, coming up to its fifth anniversary, Conrail had already gobbled up almost $3.3 billion of Federal money, and it was still losing heavily. This was much less Conrail

Above left: Norfolk Southern livery perpetuates N & W black as the basic color, but enlivens it with a nose-end prancing horse logo.

Center: These new 3,500hp SD50 diesels from GM-EMD typify the rejuvenation of Conrail's traction fleet in the 1980s.

Above right: Conrail Chairman and Chief Executive, L. Stanley Crane, sees for himself in the control tower of the railroad's big Elkhart, Indiana, classification yard.

management's fault than failures on the part of its founders. USRA, created by Congress to plot a potentially viable Northeastern rail network, then to sit at its progeny's elbow as banker and consultant, had hopelessly overestimated the likely growth of Conrail's coal tonnage by about 25 percent. That it did not foresee depression in the steel and auto industries, or the migration of heavy industry from the territory, was perhaps less culpable. Be that as it may, the combined effect was a 20 percent shortfall on USRA's projections of Conrail freight as a whole.

USRA also grossly misjudged the state of the fixed plant, traction, and freight cars which Conrail had inherited from its bankrupt forebears. In its first four years Conrail had to lay 3,873 miles of new rail, replace 18.4 million ties, resurface over 35,500 miles of track, buy 675 new locomotives, put 3,110 more through a heavy overhaul, purchase 8,136 new freight cars and treat over 73,000 more to heavy repairs before it could fully satisfy its shippers.

Conrail itself was slow to tackle the oversized network it had been handed;

and because its hauls were short by comparison with those of other big Class I systems, the cost of its excess of terminals loomed large in its balance sheet. But it was not easy to prune the overlapping facilities of the pre-Conrail system, or to develop new strategies based on a slimmed down network, when Conrail had been forced to cede extravagant job concessions to the staff it had taken over. Those concessions had saddled Conrail with ratio of labor costs to total operating expenses way above the Class I norm. Finally, Conrail's founders had required it to continue the city commuter operations of its predecessors, on terms that were far from meeting the losses these passenger services incurred.

To the incoming Reagan Administration at the start of 1981, the Conrail concept was clearly anathema. Its immediate aim of a fire sale was frustrated by Congress, but the legislature had obviously to take some remedial action. The outcome was the Northeast Rail Services Act (NERSA) of 1981.

Regional transportation authorities were ordered to take over the commuter services by the start of 1983, or else contract with a newborn Amtrak subsidiary for their assumption. In the event the Amtrak subsidiary was stillborn. Each commuter operation was taken over locally – though not without traumas, as some of the authorities had to withstand protracted labor walkouts before they could impose more realistic pay-scales and terms than those in which the men had luxuriated under Conrail.

But on Conrail itself NERSA rescinded the very indulgent job protection clauses written into the system's initial constitution. Conrail was further required to sell off all its lines in Connecticut and Rhode Island, and in part of Massachusetts. Finally, Conrail was given until mid-1983 to prove to USRA that it had the capability to be viable. If it passed that test, NERSA bound the Administration to seek a buyer for Conrail as an intact railroad, not take the easy course of selling Conrail's most profitable segments piecemeal.

At the beginning of 1981 Conrail took on a new Chairman, former Southern Railway executive L Stanley Crane. Under him Conrail staged an extraordinary turnround. First, in May 1981, Conrail's employees were coaxed into wage increase concessions which gave impetus to the Congressional enactment of NERSA, and which promised to yield the railroad some $350 million savings up to mid-1984. Then NERSA's revision of employee terms of service, substituting the once-for-all-time Federally-funded severance payments for the original long-term wage or job guarantees, freed Conrail to start the overdue rationalization of its route system. By 1982, in a first-phase scheme branded "Window I," abandonment applications had been filed for no fewer than 360 superfluous and profitless branch-line segments aggregating 2,607 miles; by the 1983-84 winter 1,777 miles had been discarded or approved for abandonment by the ICC, and 765 miles had been sold off to short lines (of which more later) or others for

continued operation. In the spring of 1984 Central had a further 431 segments of line totaling 1,641 miles tabled for disposal as generating insufficient revenue, under the "Window II" continuation of the rationalization drive.

Meanwhile the massive plant and rolling stock rehabilitation program launched at Conrail's inception, which seasoned observers acknowledged was creating some of the most handsomely manicured main-line track in the country, had been complemented by innovative marketing and such discrimination in favor of the best-paying traffic as a US railroad's common carrier obligations decently allowed. Conrail had begun life with some 8,000 miles of its network subject to slow orders because of inferior track. By the end of 1983 the total had been trimmed to a mere 200 miles or so on the core trunk network, and 2,600 route-miles elsewhere. Most of the main lines had been relaid with continuous welded rail which was continuous on the ex-New York Central's so-called Water Level Route from New York to Chicago via Albany, Buffalo, Cleveland, and Toledo. Concentration on high-volume flows had made Conrail's dedicated Trailvan intermodal trains, up to 36 of them daily, conveying piggy-back trailers and maritime containers between its 34 eastern and midwestern terminals, one of the territory's showpieces.

The pay-off started to show in 1981, when Conrail posted the first, if very modest, full-year net income in its short history. Thereafter the surplus climbed steadily, scaling $313 million on re-

venues of $3,076 million in 1983, and on the outcome of 1984's first three-quarters promising close to $500 million for that year. Since June 1981, moreover, Conrail had not had to seek any Federal money. It has been able to secure its capital investment needs in the private sector (though by the end of 1983, admittedly, its drawings there had topped $1 billion).

So it was as an integral concern that the DOT put Conrail on the market in 1984. The 14 bids submitted by the mid-June deadline included offers from CSX, NS, the Allegheny Corporation (onetime controllers of New York Central) and a New England railroad conglomerate this chapter has yet to discuss, Guildford Transportation Industries (GTI). By the fall, the Department of Transportation had given a thumbs-down to 11 of the contestants and short-listed NS (despite initial coolness to Conrail's acquisition by another railroad), the Allegheny Corporation and another financial group fronted by international hotelier J Willard Marriott. The bidders frozen out included Conrail's own staff, but at the end of October Conrail responded with a proposal which, with a cash offer of $1.4 billion, topped those already on the table; Conrail aimed to fund its offer partly with its own dollars, partly by a bank loan, and partly by a common stock flotation. The Department's reaction was very dismissive, but then a political ground-swell of antipathy to a quick sale of Conrail to another party was detectable. Conrail's fresh attempt to keep the system under its existing

Top left: Three of the Alaska Railroad's GM-EMD GP49 diesels.

Center left: Alaska Railroad passenger equipment includes ten dome cars acquired secondhand from the Milwaukee, Denver & Rio Grande Western, and Canadian railroads.

Left: A regular rail barge service spans the 1,300 miles of sea from the Alaska railroad at Whittier to the rest of the US rail system at Seattle, or to the Canadian rail system at Prince Rupert, British Columbia.

management had the support of both Pennsylvania's republican senators.

The Reagan Administration was also divesting itself of the Alaska Railroad, the core of which was constructed in 1913-23 with Federal money to link up two existing short lines in the Seward and Fairbanks areas. In the 1970s the railroad's carrying slumped and it slipped into losses when completion of the Alaska pipeline ended a bonanza of construction materials traffic. But by 1983 both passenger and freight business had rebounded to record levels, benefitting moreover from a railroad that was in good shape because of the shrewd investment of pipeline era profits in track and rolling stock upgrading. The outlook was brighter yet, thanks to a contract with South Korean interests for unit train movement of coal 360 miles from a mine at Healey to a new transshipment terminal at the port of Seward (the first deep-draft installation of this kind on the US west coast, incidentally), and also to developing intermodal traffic in roll-on/roll-off barges with Seattle via the two Alaskan ports of Seward and Whittier. Transfer of the railroad to the state of Alaska for $22.3 million was to be completed by January 1985.

The least expected early-1980 move on the merger scene was the successful bid of multimillionaire Timothy Mellon to mold into a single, 4,050-mile system three smaller railroads twined among the giants of the Northeast from Maryland to the Canadian border.

The investment hardly looked gilt-edged, since two of the systems, the Boston & Maine and Delaware & Hudson, were financially embarrassed (there had been some Congressional effort to propel both into Conrail in the run-up to NERSA's 1981 passage). Furthermore, all three were operating in territory where hauls were comparatively short and trucking competition consequently vicious. But Mellon was convinced such deterrents were outweighed by the traffic prospects of a rationalized single system in the region. "The times are such that rail-

roads are more and more important in terms of the economic viability of this country," he wrote in 1981. "They seem like a good investment."

In June 1981 Mellon opened his account with purchase by his Guildford Transportation Industries (GTI) of the 817-mile Maine Central. Then, after negotiation of Boston & Maine's debts with the bankruptcy court, that railroad was absorbed by GTI in June 1983 and the Delaware & Hudson at the start of 1984. The three railroads have retained their individual identities, but they are under the command of the same chief executive and are operated as a unified network, with interchangeability of locomotives.

GTI's future prospects could be clouded by a sale of Conrail. Its east-west trade is reliant on trackage rights to Newark (NJ), Buffalo, Philadelphia, and Washington over Conrail metals which were captured by GTI's Delaware & Hudson constituent at Conrail's birth. Without them, D&H, left to the limited potential of its own thin stem from the Canadian border through Albany to eastern Pennsylvania, would surely have foundered. A new Conrail owner would probably hike the rental for those rights. But if the buyer were NS, it would freeze out GTI and keep its New England traffic on its own trains right to Albany. If that eventuated, depriving GTI of some 600 freight carloads a day, GTI's Chief Executive has conceded that he "would have to fold up the tent at D&H."

While GTI was taking shape, a mas-

Above: A Maine Central GP38 prepares to leave Bangor, Maine, yard with a morning freight for the Canadian border.

sive regrouping of railroads in the western US had reached its conclusion. Union Pacific had betrayed no ambitions to expand since its second thoughts in the early 1970s about strengthening its Midwestern presence through acquisition of the hapless Chicago, Rock Island & Pacific – the "Rock." With the non-rail activity of its parent corporation generating more than half the latter's revenue and attracting about 60 percent of its investment, it seemed unlikely that UP would want to extend its commitment to railroading. Besides, the existing 9,420-mile UP network, joining limbs from Los Angeles and Seattle/Portland into a double-track main from Ogden to Omaha that was arguably, in relation to its length, the busiest rail freight highway in the whole country, already boasted the longest average freight hauls in the US. Married to UP's traditionally efficient operating method, that made the railroad look nicely contoured for profit as it was.

Early in 1980, however, UP stunned its railroad neighbors by announcing that, after negotiations which – no less surprisingly – had been kept a hermetically-sealed secret from the rest of the industry, it had concluded an agreement in principle to take over the 11,277-mile Missouri Pacific, along with that company's subsidiary gas exploration, production, and pipeline

interests. The price was around $1 billion. Then, just two weeks later, it bid a further $25 million for the 1,482-mile Western Pacific. With Missouri Pacific, or the "Mo-Pac," UP's empire would reach further east to Chicago and St Louis, and drive a broad wedge southward through Kansas, Missouri, Oklahoma, and Arkansas to El Paso, Laredo, and Houston in Texas, and to New Orleans. Western Pacific would give it direct access from Salt Lake City to Oakland and San Francisco, in parallel with Southern Pacific.

The shock waves from these proposals naturally whipped up strong reaction from anxious neighbors, mostly expressed in the usual demands for extravagant trackage rights over parts of the mega-system to offset the latter's breakout from the historic UP midwest gateway of Council Bluffs, Indiana, Kansas City, and Ogden, Utah. But Santa Fe strove to block the alliance completely as fundamentally inimical to the public interest, however indulgently it was circumscribed by grants of trackage rights to adjacent railroads. However, in approving BN's takeover of the Frisco the ICC had shown it was far less susceptible than it had been in mid-century to exorbitant trackage rights

claims, and to threats that their refusal would condemn the appellants to creeping penury. Late in 1982 it endorsed the consolidation of the three railroads with a rider agreeing only a proportion of the trackage right demands, principally those of Southern Pacific (Kansas-St Louis), Denver & Rio Grande Western (Pueblo-Kansas City) and Missouri-Kansas-Texas, the "Katy" (Kansas City-Omaha/Council Bluffs, Lincoln and Topeka). Shortly afterwards Santa Fe, Kansas City Southern, Denver & Rio Grande Western, and Southern Pacific had their appeals against the ICC rulings rejected by the US Supreme Court and the merger became effective on 22 December 1981.

Western Pacific was subsequently absorbed as a fourth UP operating district, but UP and Mo-Pac have preserved their separate identities, though they are now promoted as one enterprise under the Union Pacific System brand and their locomotives are all taking on the traditional UP Armor yellow color scheme. The three traffic departments have been merged for development and marketing of the combined network as a unitary system, with common operating, service, and pricing policies.

With the BN-Frisco and UP System alliances sealing off respectively the northern and central regions of the western US, defensive action by one or more of the remaining railroads in the area was a certainty. It came in May 1980, but in a form none had anticipated: an announcement by traditional antagonists Santa Fe and Southern Pacific that their two boards had agreed in principle to SP's absorption by Santa Fe.

Above left: The engineer mounts the lead SD40-2 of a UP System Oakland, California—Midwest run-through freight at North Platte, Nebraska. The train will deliver its intermodal cargo in 18 hours less than the norm before the Union Pacific/Missouri Pacific merger.

Above: A Union Pacific snowplow carves a path through formidable drifts between Ashton and Tetonia, Idaho, in April 1982.

Top right: A celebrated Union Pacific location, the Keddie Wye junction in California, with four of UP's heavily predominant road-haul power type, the GM-EMD SD40-2.

Right: A Southern Pacific train of export coal heads for a northern Californian port west of Reno, Nevada.

Santa Fe's assumption of lead role was surprising. It had evinced no enthusiasm for aggrandizement since the start of the century and seemed content with its southwestern span of the US from San Francisco, Los Angeles and San Diego to Chicago, Kansas City, Dallas, and Houston. Though its anxiety at the UP-MoPac-WP alliance had been expressed in court action, Santa Fe had seemed initially prepared to ride the consequences of that merger if its litigation failed.

SP, on the other hand, was in 1980 seeking a firmer bridgehead in the Midwest. Its network fringing the Pacific coast and the Mexican border from Portland through San Francisco, Los Angeles, Tucson, and El Paso round to Dallas, Houston, and New Orleans was projected on to Memphis and St Louis over the metals of what was legally its principal subsidiary, the Cotton Belt Railroad (officially the St Louis Southwestern, but rarely dignified with that title). However, the "Cotton Belt" lettering of the subsidiary's vehicles is nowadays the only evidence that it is treated as anything but an SP operating division. To add Midwestern access to the SP system, the Cotton Belt in 1980 bought the bankrupt Rock Island's 973-

25

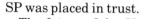

mile line from Santa Rosa, New Mexico, through Kansas City to St Louis; and SP promptly put in hand a $97 million rehabilitation of its Tucumcari-Topeka stretch to restore fitness for 60mph freight operations, then bargained trackage rights over MoPac from Kansas City to St Louis. All this would have SP equipped with a transcontinental route to St Louis some 400 miles shorter than its previous, circuitous approach.

It was not a scheme calculated to delight competitor Santa Fe, already well-placed to handle transcontinental freight between the Pacific coast and the Midwest. Nor did SP dump its plan to redevelop the Rock Island share of what was known as the Golden State Route when the merger move was agreed. That was undoubtedly one fac-

tor in the May 1980 collapse of the discussions with Santa Fe. In any event, there was skepticism abroad that the ICC would approve a merger which concentrated in one conglomerate 5,388 of the 7,244 rail route-miles in California.

Mature consideration of the effects of the UP-MoPac-WP merger prompted second thoughts. In September 1983 Santa Fe and SP announced that they had settled their differences and agreed to combine under the aegis of a holding company ponderously titled the Santa Fe Southern Pacific Corporation. In the resultant 25,200-mile system Santa Fe would have the majority, 54 percent share. The marriage was effected at the end of 1983, but pending ICC approval, sought the following March, the stock of

SP was placed in trust.

The future of the Class I railroads so far untouched by the mega-system mergers was the topic absorbing analysts of the US railroad scene. Illinois Central Gulf's openness to offers has already been mentioned. Expectedly, another railroad to announce early in 1984 that it was seeking a buyer was Denver & Rio Grande, dwarfed by surrounding BN and UP System – and, furthermore, since 1969 only a component of an expanding conglomerate, Rio Grande Industries.

The focus of interest in 1984 was the Midwest. One bankrupt, the Rock Island, had already been dismantled and its worthwhile segments sold off to neighbors or to new short line companies. The remaining question was who would get the Chicago, Milwaukee, St Paul & Pacific, more compactly known as the Milwaukee Road, which had survived two bankruptcies, in 1921 and 1935, more or less unscathed, but not yet one more insolvency in 1977. The reorganization by a trusteeship ensuing from this final debacle had shorn the Milwaukee of all its western territory, which once reached Tacoma in Washington state, and pared it down from 9,800 to only some 3,800 route-miles interconnecting Chicago, Kansas City, Minneapolis/St Paul, and (via trackage rights over other roads) Duluth and Louisville. For purchase of that rump Chicago & North Western, Soo Line, and Grand Trunk Western were in contention.

Grand Trunk Western (GTW) is a Canadian property, the chief constituent of the Grand Trunk Corporation set up in 1970 to gather in the US subsidiaries of the state-owned Canadian National (CN); its other constituents are the Duluth, Winnipeg & Pacific (DWP) and Central Vermont (CV), neither qualifying for Class I status. CV has been badly pinched both by the consolidation of neighboring New England systems in Mellon's GTI and by the sharper competition arising from deregulation, so much so that in 1982 CN was trying to sell CV off, but

stepped in. The interest of Soo Line – or, to be pedantic, the Minneapolis, Sault St Marie & Atlantic, though few people nowadays are aware of the full title – was foreseeable. For one thing, Soo parallels the Milwaukee in the Chicago-Minneapolis/St Paul-Duluth region. For another, it is a subsidiary of CN's great rival on the Canadian system's home ground, Canadian Pacific (CP). The 4,433-mile Soo derives a major part of its income from maritime container traffic shipped through Canadian ports on the St Lawrence Seaway.

The 8,200-mile Chicago & North Western, the third bidder, is also a near carbon copy of the Chicago-Milwaukee-Twin Cities-Duluth area, beyond which it reaches south to Kansas City and St Louis, and west through Omaha and across Nebraska and South Dakota into Wyoming. Thus it is affected not only by the future of the residual Milwaukee system but also by some of the mega-railroad groupings already described. Since 1980 CNW has already developed its presence in the Midwest by taking over some 800 miles of the defunct Rock Island's trackage, including RI's Kansas City-Twin Cities main line, and about 150 miles of Milwaukee grain-gathering branches in Iowa. In 1983-84 CNW was embarked on a $57 million scheme to hoist the capacity of the ex-RI Kansas City-Twin Cities single track to

then withdrew it from the market the following year.

GTW runs a main line from Port Huron (Mich) on the Great Lake of that name to Chicago and another south through Detroit to Jackson (Mich), enjoying access from the latter to Cincinnati and exchanges there with Seaboard and Southern through trackage rights from Conrail. It has been on an expansionist tack in the 1980s. From less than 1,000, GTW's route-mileage has jumped to 1,699, largely through 1980 acquisition of the 478-mile Detroit, Toledo & Ironton (DTI) – its present Detroit-Jackson line – and of Conrail's discarded Michigan trackage. As a result it has lately adopted the more opulent title of Grand Trunk Rail System. If the Milwaukee were tacked on to this network, Grand Trunk would have commanded a seamless system right around the south of Lake Michigan, would improve its net income through longer average freight hauls, and not least would tap business to reduce the extent of its present dependence for freight on the erratically-performing automotive industry.

For a while Grand Trunk's bid for the Milwaukee looked unchallenged and the two systems had already launched collaborative exercises when rivals

Far left, top: Cotton Belt is the commonly used title of the St Louis Southwestern, a subsidiary of Southern Pacific that preserves its separate identity.

Far left, below: Five Denver & Rio Grande Western SD40s wheel 73 carloads of coal over the Craig branch, in northwestern Colorado, to Denver.

Above: The final livery of the Milwaukee Road, acquired in 1985 by Soo Line after a bidding contest with Chicago & North Western.

Below: UP and Chicago & North Western SD40-2s link couplers to hoist an eastbound freight up Echo Canyon, Utah.

20 million gross tons annually, but its major enterprise in 1984 was completion of a scheme for greater participation in coal movement out of Wyoming.

The state of Milwaukee Road play in the fall of 1984 was that the ICC had stated a preference for Soo ownership, but CNW had tabled the highest bid. If CNW won, it was certain to adopt the Milwaukee as its prime Chicago-Twin Cities route, since that threaded more commercially fruitful areas than its own. However, neither CNW or Soo would get as appealing a Milwaukee as they first thought. Defeated GTW reacted to this snub by switching to Burlington Northern the heavy traffic which since 1982, anticipating a smooth Milwaukee takeover of its own, it had been channeling on to the Milwaukee in Chicago. The 49,000 carloads a year that represented was widely credited as the force behind the sharply contracted Milwaukee's return to the black.

Another Class I railroad with a keen interest in the Powder River basin is the 1,663-mile Kansas City Southern (KCS), which mates with BN to ferry coal from Wyoming to utilities in Arkansas, Louisiana, and Texas. KCS, which includes the Louisiana & Arkansas, is a slender chord south from Kansas City to Port Arthur, Texas, and New Orleans, with an offshoot to Dallas by grace of Santa Fe trackaging rights. Thus it has been in the thick of the mega-system mergers of the 1980s. But so far the diversified conglomerate of which it is a subsidiary, Kansas City Southern Industries, has seemed relatively unmoved.

Equally menaced by the BN/Frisco and UP-MoPac mergers was the Missouri-Kansas-Texas (MKT), generally known as the "Katy," which operates from Kansas City and St Louis in the north down through Oklahoma to Dallas, Forth Worth, San Antonio, and Galveston in Texas. It is another beneficiary of the Rock Island break-up, and operates some 600 former "Rock" route-miles focussed on the bankrupt's Salina (Kansas)-Dallas line under its Oklahoma & Texas Railroad subsidiary.

"Katy's" traffic is naturally dominated by shipment freight to and from the southern ports, with coal and grain outstanding. Although, as remarked earlier, it has conceded trackage rights over MoPac to Lincoln, Omaha and Council Bluffs, and west to Topeka, to preserve its vital northern connections in face of the UP-Mopac merger, "Katy" has been penalized by shut-out from other routes and gateways as a result of mergers; and also, as already mentioned, by the pinching of its rates as the new giants set their single-system tariffs for traffic to and from "Katy" territory which they were obviously reluctant to match in joint rates for freight channeled through the "Katy" routes.

Of the remaining small Class I railroads, four are locked into the steel industry and consequently debilitated by the latter's depression. The 273-mile Pittsburgh & Lake Erie, which shares with Chessie and Conrail ownership of the 136-mile Monongahela Railway (or Monon) on the borders of Pennsylvania and West Virginia, counts three-quarters of its traffic in raw material and finished product transport for the steel industry. Substantial 1970s investment in anticipation of traffic that did not materialize has saddled P&LE with serious debt and in the early 1980s it was working in the red, at an operating ratio worse than 125 percent.

The other three steel-based systems are in fact owned by the United States Steel Corporation, which following its costly 1982 purchase of Marathon Oil announced that it was open to offers for any or all of them. So far there have been no takers. The three railroads are: the 205-mile Bessemer & Lake Erie, from the Pittsburgh area to Conneaut on Lake Erie; the 357-mile Duluth, Missabe & Iron Range, the major ore carrier among US railroads, ferrying the mineral from the Missabe range in northeastern Minnesota to ports at the western end of Lake Superior; and the 231-mile Elgin, Joliet & Eastern, which traces a semicircle around Chicago, from Waukegan (Ill) on Lake Michigan to Porter (Ind), with a key branch to the US steel plant at Gary (Ind), and which in the course of that arc intersects every railroad serving Chicago.

The one jaunty system among the smaller Class Is is the iconoclastic Flor-

ida East Coast (FCE), the 554-mile railroad fringing the Atlantic coast from Jacksonville down to Miami. Its boldness in opting out of the industry-wide pay negotiation system in 1963 and determination to break the mold of anachronistic work rules, which committed it to eight years increasingly bitter confrontation with the labor unions, has already been outlined. The reward of its obduracy is striking.

Able to run trains the whole length of its main line with a two-man crew, instead of halting them twice en route for changes of the once mandatory five-man crews – and, incidentally, running the trains without cabooses, an economy to which other railroads did not win labor consent until 1982 – FCE can schedule its freights at an average speed of almost 40mph. It can also afford to run trains of no more than 15-20 cars to keep both loads and returning empties flowing continuously day and night. The pay-off is that though FCE competes in all its prime traffic centers with the far bigger Seaboard System arm of mighty CSX, it turned in the best operating ratio (80.2

percent) of all Class I railroads in 1984. FCE is also as high as eighth in the intermodal league in terms of annual carloadings, even though its main line is only some 350 miles long.

To deal adequately with the many US railroads not aspiring to Class I status would need a book twice the size of this one. Some of them are very sizeable enterprises. The Providence & Worcester, for example, is a 371-mile system in New England, while the Bangor & Aroostook extends for 494 miles from north to south of Maine.

At the bottom end of US railroading scale is the most rapidly expanding type of system in recent years – the shortline. In 1984 the shortline total was over 400, with an average length of less than 30 miles.

The great majority of shortlines have been created to serve shippers and industries not directly connected to a major railroad, and which a local company with modest overheads can achieve more economically than its big neighbors. (But it follows, of course, that shortline is very dependent on the service and rates it gets from the major

railroad – or railroads – into which it feeds for its prosperity.) Besides scope to adopt more flexible work-rule, a short-line scores over a bigger carrier by striking up closer relationships with its clients, and by stimulating a degree of local support that can open up local industrial development funds for its use.

In the 3R and 4R Acts, Congress acted to safeguard existing shortlines and encourage new ones with the offer of start-up subsidies. The Reagan Administration, however, shut off Federal funding and now shortline aid is derived chiefly from state or local agencies and shippers groups. Many recent additions to the shortline total are takeovers of branches discarded as uneconomic by the major railroads. The NERSA legislation of 1981, by permitting Conrail to put its redundant branches on the market at rock-bottom prices, alone promoted creation of 21 new shortlines, which in concert with 57 already in existence, kept alive 591 miles of the trackage Conrail had to abandon as unremunerative. Conrail now regards these shortlines as invaluable retailers of its trunk service.

3
THE UNIT FREIGHT TRAIN TO INTEGRAL FREIGHT TRAIN

Just over one in four loaded US freight cars carries coal, which is by far the railroads' biggest single generator of tonnage. In the early 1980s annual car loadings were hovering around the 5.2–5.6 million mark, out of a total for all freight of between 18.5 and 19 million. Next behind coal came intermodal traffic, climbing steadily beyond the 2 million annual carloadings mark, followed by grain at 1.25–1.4 million and chemicals at 1.1–1.2 million.

Almost two-thirds of all coal dug in the US is lifted from the mines by rail. The railroads have retained this dominance of the market because economy of the train as a bulk haulier has been further improved since the middle of this century through the increasing concentration of tonnage into unit trains that are worked intact, without any re-sorting of their cars en route, from source to user. In fact, the cost of long-haul coal transportation by rail has been decreasing in real money terms: certainly actual rail rates have these past ten years advanced less sharply than the cost of the coal itself at source.

Thus the railroads are the natural choice for bulk coal movement, except where inland waterways permit multi-barge operation, of which the 30-barge trains seen on the Lower Mississippi are an extreme example: barge operators have a bonus in that they pay far less toward the upkeep cost of their highways than a railroad does. The biggest threat to rail supremacy has been the slurry pipeline, but the growth of this mode has been kept in check partly by the first cost of pipeline installation, partly by environmental opposition, and not least by railroads' refusal to allow pipelines to cross their tracks and their adroit maneuvering in Washington to prevent an embargo on

such stonewalling.

However, because rail has such a grip on bulk coal transportation, it was coal that raised the temperature of the 1979–80 Washington debate on deregulation. Mining and public utility interests came close to scuppering the Staggers Bill altogether in their bitter fight for a much lower ceiling on the margins the railroads could claim on their direct coal-hauling costs than the Staggers Act eventually permitted. Those same interests were in the forefront of agitation for the Staggers amendment in the mid-1980s, despite the ability of some major coal-hauling railroads to show that they had not taken full advantage of the scope handed them by Staggers to increase their prices.

Rail movement of coal has increased rapidly since the early 1970s, though not quite to the extent some analysts were forecasting a few years ago, largely because of the global economic recession. Burlington Northern, for example, lifted only 17 million tons from seams in its territory in 1970, but in the 1980s its annual gross has been more than 100 million tons. The cause, of course, is increased resort to coal fuel in export markets as well as at home, since oil prices took to the stratosphere after OPEC was jolted by the 1973 Arab-Israeli war into appreciation of its powerful position.

Four factors have brought about marked changes in the pattern of rail coal movement since the 1960s. One has been the rising demand for cleaner-burning low-sulfur coal from the Midwest fields in states such as Wyoming and Montana since the 1970 Clean Air

Right: Seaboard System unit coal train.

Left: One method of rapid mineral wagon discharge; this Strachan & Henshaw tipper at the Massey coal terminal, Newport News, Virginia, rotates two cars simultaneously and can discharge up to 60 cars an hour.

Right: A 110-car Burlington Northern coal train loads at a mine near Gillette, Wyoming: loading proceeds with the train continuously at walking pace and will be completed within two hours.

Below right: A GM-EMD SD50 in the stark white styling of Kansas City Southern.

Act – the prime reason for the upsurge in BN's coal traffic. A second has been the climb of US coal exports, a third the conversion of public utilities and industrial plants from oil, though this has not been at the pace anticipated when the Carter Administration preached a changeover gospel so ardently in the wake of the oil price explosion and OPEC's oil embargos. Finally, the railroads have been able to match up many of the new coal consumers economically with remote sources through the developing efficiency of their unit train method, coupled with provision of high-performance rapid train loading and discharge installations at minehead and delivery point.

As an example of the considerable restructure of coal flows, take the Louisville & Nashville constituent of what is now the Seaboard System. In the 1960s roughly three-quarters of the coal lifted by L&N from the eastern Kentucky field traveled northward to Great Lakes consumers on amicably graded double-track routes. A decade or more later, with L&N's annual coal tonnage already 25 percent higher, the same proportion was streaming southward to Gulf Coast utilities or docks for export. On top of dire problems in rustling up enough cars to absorb the mounting tonnage, L&N had to grapple with operating on fiercely graded, generally single-track lines through the Appalachians that were unfit for

such a throughput. One such line had its traffic expand by no less than two-thirds in ten years. To still the raucous outcry from customers whose coal shipments were chronically disrupted by track flaws on these new routes, and by shortages of traction and cars, L&N was compelled in 1978 to order a $73 million emergency program of track works and to lay out $350 million on new locomotives and coal cars.

That was pre-Staggers. At that period the ICC's clamp on coal rates was allowing the railroads no more than a 7 percent margin or thereabouts on the roughly attributed direct costs of moving the tonnage. Small wonder, then, that the Staggers Act stressed the railroads' need for a better return if they were to undertake the essential renewal of assets and capacity expansion to absorb the anticipated growth of traffic efficiently. L&N had to coax assent out of the ICC to a unique 22 percent hike of its coal rates before it could commit itself to that 1978 expenditure.

Burlington Northern, too, had to be blunt to get a fair return on its new coal business. The deals it had struck with public utilities for coal shipments from the developing Powder River basin on the Wyoming-Montana border had foreseen neither the general cost inflation following the 1974 oil crisis nor the extent of track work it would face to fit

routes out of the territory of the stresses of heavy coal trains. Between 1976 and 1981 BN plowed no less than 55 cents of every dollar it invested into locomotives, cars, and more particularly track projects to cater for coal – in all, a total of $1.1 billion. In the end, despite managing to impose some modest rate increases, BN's return on coal movement was so meager that it had to back its insistence on comprehensive renegotiations of the contracts with a threat to close its treasury completely to further investment in the business unless its clients saw reason.

The centerpiece of BN's investment was the 625-mile route out of the Powder River field at Gillette, Wyoming, to Lincoln, Nebraska, the outlet for coal heading to the Midwest and the Sunbelt. This was originally a secondary route of BN's constituent, the Chicago, Burlington & Quincy, which was largely single-track and in the 1960s burdened with no more than 8 million tons of freight a year. Now parts of it were required to channel an eightfold increase and process a dozen or more lengthy trains each way every weekday.

The biggest single project was construction of a brand-new, 116-mile line south from Gillette to (Bell Ayr) to Orin, which both shortened the route from the coalfield to the south by some 155 miles and also tapped new coal deposits on the rim of the Powder River basin. This was the longest stretch of new rail route laid in the US since 1931. In addition, several new branches

were put down to mines, raising the total of new track installed to over 180 miles. Over the rest of the route to Lincoln – and subsequently over a further 390 miles to Kansas City – the line was completely rebuilt with continuously-welded, heavy duty 132lb/yd rail, bridges were reconstructed for greater strength and ten-mile long passing loops added at intervals. The considerable length of these loops contributed valuably to the expansion of operating capacity because with Centralized Traffic Control (CTC) – discussed in Chapter 5 – under the hand of adept dispatchers and radio communication between them and train crews, train speeds could be regulated so that opposing hauls always crossed each other well inside the loop area; thus neither train was halted during the meet. All this improvement was topped off by erection of a new diesel locomotive and car maintenance and servicing shop roughly midway between Gillette and Lincoln at Alliance, Nebraska; and not least by acquisition of over 750 new locomotives and 2,500 freight cars specifically for coal service.

Another new access to the Powder River Basin coalfield was commissioned in 1984. Chicago & North Western once aimed to make its own penetration, but the ICC demurred on environmental grounds and ordained that CNW combine with BN in a joint, single-access scheme, the Gillette-Orin line. But BN had to finish that on its own because of finance problems on CNW's side. There followed complex fund-raising, litigation, and negotiation moves which culminated in a joint Union Pacific-CNW scheme, "Project Yellow." This involved construction of 56 miles of new railroad from the UP south of the coalfield at South Morrill to link with neglected CNW trackage east of Orin, which was rehabilitated; and the welding of this into BN's Gillette-Orin line, terms for CNW's joint use of which were renegotiated successfully. In its entirety Project Yellow ran up a bill of £445 million.

Latter-day preoccupation with track

strength on key coal routes arises because of the anxiety to shift more coal per train-mile in view of the comparatively low rates railroads can charge per ton moved. In the past decade and a half this has led to virtual standardization of the "100-tonner" coal gondola or hopper, so tagged because its payload capacity is around 100 tons. But its all-up weight is around 120 tons, so that each and every axle is laying at least 32 tons weight on the track and its foundations.

The stress is very demanding when that 32 tons' pressure is repeated 400 times by the 100-car coal drags run by several roads, with the addition of impact from three or four muscular six-motored-axle diesels. On vital coal arteries like those out of the Powder River Basin the tracks, as already indicated, will be taking that pounding from loaded trains a dozen or more times a day.

No one dreams now of easing gross car weights. The next move for a better margin on the coal-haul job will be in pursuit of bigger payloads per ton of car weight. Some modest advances have been secured without departure from all-steel production, but the biggest improvements are to be seen in new designs with light-alloy car bodies.

The resilience of this kind of coal car to all the strains and stresses of con-

tinuous heavy-haul rail work was proven by a prototype car, the Algola, built to a technique originated by the European company Alusuisse, which triumphantly underwent many thousands of miles' service proving on Burlington Northern and Santa Fe in the early 1980s. It offers a 10 percent better payload/empty weight ratio than most steel-bodied cars: and that, besides adding over 1,000 tons of coal to the gross of a 100-car train, also implies usefully trimmed operating costs over a round trip, because the empty train's weight is reduced and consequently needs less diesel horsepower to return the cars to the mines.

Other companies offering new aluminum-bodied models in 1984 included Ortner and Pullman Standard/Trinity Industries. The latter's design, with an empty weight of less than 20 tons, could be loaded with up to 111 tons of coal: in addition, careful attention to shaping was claimed to make it 60 percent more aerodynamically efficient than contemporary steel-bodied types, so that a full train should exact less fuel consumption from its locomotives. Nevertheless, up to the end of 1984 there was no sign of other coal consumers or railroads queuing up to follow the lead of the Southern California utility, Santee Cooper, in placing with Portec, US licensee of the Alusuisse technique, an

Above left: Chessie System's prototype lightweight, pod-bottom coal car.

Above: This hopper for plastic pellets by National Steel Car of Canada has one of the largest cubic load capacities yet attained in an eight-wheel car.

Above right: The prototype aluminum-bodied coal car was subjected to exhaustive service testing by Santa Fe.

Below right: Six Santa Fe SD40-2s, with a gross output of 18,000hp, front this westbound unit coal train near Flagstaff on a wintry day in Arizona.

order for 300 cars based on the Algola demonstrator.

Unit train working from source to consumer dominates coal haulage nowadays. Seaboard System, for example, despatches that way three-quarters of the coal mined on its territory in Kentucky, Tennessee, southwest Virginia, Alabama, Indiana, and Illinois; its total of unit trains run in 1983 was over 6,300. Three-quarters of the tonnage was destined for utilities in the Southeast, Midwest, and along the Gulf coast.

The character of the routes traversed by many Seaboard trains, discussed earlier, counsels a maximum loading of 90 cars, but some other coal hauliers, such as Burlington Northern, run consists of up to 110 cars with a payload of

some 9,800 tons and a gross weight behind the locomotives of over 12,800 tons. The interstate distances traveled are often formidable. BN, for instance, has a regular run of 1,688 miles from the Spring Creek Mine in Montana to Smithers Lake, Texas. The longest unit train circuit so far recorded is one of 2,073 miles, no less, from a Utah mine to a Mississippi utility.

The unit train principle and its improved operational economy, backed up by 1980s ability to cut contractual deals, have given the rails a firmer hold on other bulk commodity markets – grain, for instance. A 10,000-ton unit train of grain forging from the Midwest to a Gulf Coast port is as common a sight in season on Illinois Gulf Central tracks as a block of Illinois-mined coal heading for a foreign consumer.

The Illinois Central component of ICG was effectively the pioneer of the unit grain train, in a "Rent-a-Train" idea it sold to the big farm produce company, Cargill Inc, way back in 1967. Honored by the Chicago press of the day with the headlines such as "Move over, Avis" and "For the shipper who has everything," the scheme made an 86-hopper train available exclusively to Cargill at an annual rental fee plus modest ton-mile royalty on traffic moved, for grain bound from central Illinois to the Gulf. On that basis Cargill paid roughly a third of the conventional per-bushel rate for rail transport from Iowa to the Gulf.

Union Pacific adopted unit train

practice for grain in the mid-1970s, followed by other roads including Missouri Pacific, Santa Fe, and Chessie. Burlington Northern launched its first modest unit grain train program late in 1980 and within three years had converted over 60 percent of its total grain movement to the format. On UP the proportion moving by train is around 45 percent.

However grain is not so easily adaptable to the unit train principle as bulk minerals like coal or ore, which a single source can present in enough volume to fill a 100-car train. Grain producers have to be persuaded to cooperate to get the benefit of very competitive unit train rates, by ferrying their output to a central high-capacity elevator installation – or by concentrating the stock of small elevators eventually in one major elevator.

Even so UP and BN, for example, have to be content to base their operation on units of around 25 cars only. These two railroads tend to work in multiples of around 25 cars, because that simplifies optimal rostering of locomotives to grain traffic. UP, however, consolidates these 25-car blocks into at least 50-car and mostly 75-car consists for the main-line haul out of the Midwest.

Because it is subject to less yard switching, a grain car in unit train operation achieves many more loaded journeys in a year than one in single-car working. UP has cut the previous turnround time of 26-28 days for a grain car traveling between the Midwest and California or the Northwest to a best time of 8 days. Ironically, that was aggravating one problem in 1983-84: the big nationwide surplus of grain cars since exports of wheat to Soviet

Top: A BN unit grain train, heading for a Pacific northwest port for export, crosses Gassman Coulee bridge west of Minot, North Dakota.

Center: A BN unit's grain hoppers are loaded at an elevator near Sioux City, Iowa.

Right: A line of Chesapeake & Ohio fully-enclosed tri-level auto-racks.

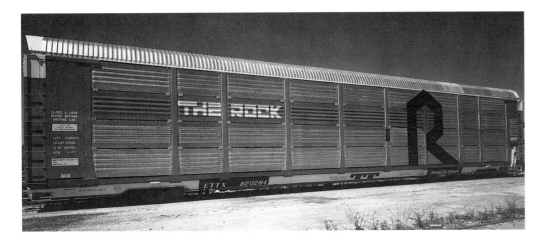

Russia were cut off and the Government offered farmers inducements to take acreage out of grain production.

The trouble was that many of the hoppers were owned or leased by the grain shippers, who wanted these used to the exclusion of railroad-owned cars: that not only left the railroads with their own cars idle and compulsion to rebate the shippers for use of the latter's cars, but landed them with expensive switching to redirect the empties to the appropriate shippers. BN eventually persuaded some shippers to accept the concept of a car pool and a general rate adjustment reflecting the number of privately-owned cars in it, so that it was no matter to a client whether his grain moved in his own hopper, someone else's or the railroad's. One should add that when, in August 1983, BN along with Soo Line found itself blessed with an alltime record month of grain car-loadings, the car pool then active did not match up: not only did cars have to be resurrected from store, but more leased from other railroads and private owners.

The savings from car pooling are valuable, but there is a much bigger bonus for any system which can drum up a back-haul traffic for the empty cars when they have discharged their grain. BN, for one, has had some success in marketing backloads of suitable granular freight, though dual-purpose use entails some modification of car loading-hatch and discharge apparatus, and of course car interior cleansing between uses. The cost of these chores is handsomely offset by the cars' additional earnings.

The more expensive the freight car, the more critical the need to keep it loaded whenever it is moving. Just about the most costly cars in North

Top left: The bulk of tri-level auto-rack is emphasised in this close-up of the Trailer Train car (photographed when on lease to the now-defunct Rock Island Railroad).

Left: Unit grain trains, too, are overhead-loaded on the move, as here on the Chessie System at Grand Ledge, Mich.

Left: General Electric C30-7s power a Seaboard unit phosphates train from central Florida's Bone Valley to Tampa port for export. Seaboard's phosphate tonnage is the biggest single rail traffic originating in Florida.
Above: Santa Fe's automobile unloading yard at Horton, Texas.
Right: One of Tampa Bay's eight big phosphate port terminals, all served by Seaboard. Again, loop layout allows trains to discharge without being broken up.

American freight operations are auto-racks, the multi-level cars with which the rails move finished vehicles from the big automotive manufacturers to distributors. A modern auto-rack is priced new at well over $100,000, because these days the auto industry is adamant that it must be fully enclosed to guard against vandalism in transit and also demands other fitments for proof against knocks and paint scarring when the auto-rack is rolling.

The railroad could not have held on to the 40-50 percent share of all new car deliveries in bulk which they won from truckers in the first half of the 1960s if they had not worked out an auto-rack pooling system with the automakers in late 1979. When each costly auto-rack had to be returned after offloading to the plant from which it originated, so it never earned revenue for 50 percent of its mileage, some railroads' auto industry business was becoming completely unprofitable.

Launched under the aegis of the Federal Railroad Administration and the Association of American Railroads (whose personnel, based in Detroit, manage the scheme), the initial pooling agreement united 16 railroads on one side and on the other Ford and General Motors, but Chrysler also joined in 1984. The total available fleet is partitioned into separate pools serving each of the three manufacturers: and within

each pool empty auto-racks are directed to the nearest plant which has a load on offer, whereas prior to the 1979 agreement they might have had an arbitrary four-figure mileage to run empty back to their loading point.

Completely flexible use of auto-racks is still out of reach. For one thing, there are two basic types, a bilevel that is generally employed to convey trucks only, and a trilevel for private cars. For another, railroads and freight car builders have yet to come up with an auto-rack that is adaptable to each of the tie-down arrangements on which the auto manufacturers individually insist to hold their products firmly damage-free within the moving rail vehicle. So at present auto-racks cannot be switched regardless from one pool to another.

Nevertheless, empty auto-rack mileages have fallen strikingly with each year of the pool's operation. GM,

for instance, reckoned it had cut out 63 million empty miles in its 1982 model year, but predicted the saving in 1984 would be 90 million. With each empty mile reckoned to cost 35 cents, the combined Ford and GM economy in 1984 was set to gross over $40 million. Since 1981, furthermore, the railroads have been able to trim their total auto-rack fleet by 12 percent and still absorb the post-recession revival of new-model auto sales.

The auto-rack fleet remains substantial, though, and in 1984 was still needing renewals on a substantial scale to cover obsolescence. In that year a total of 27 GM plants and 40 discharge terminals were served by one pool of 6,900 trilevel and 2,800 bilevel autoracks; including some installations in Canada, Ford had 15 loading and 64 offloading points using a pool of 8,745 auto-racks; and Chrysler was calling on a pool of 2,300 trilevel and 940 bilevel auto-racks to cater for nine loading and 38 offloading points. Incidentally, more than 60 percent of Ford's output leaves its plants on rail, but for GM the rail share is only 40 percent or so; it was over 50 percent in the mid-1970s.

To retain a cost-effective edge in competition with truck, barge and, in the case of some traffics, pipeline, improvement of freight car productivity

has to be a priority railroad concern. Even in unit train operation a good deal of current performance is in this respect unimpressive.

For example, in 1984 one magazine columnist dug below the euphoric print of a Norfolk Southern announcement celebrating the launch of a unit coal train flow from a West Virginian mine at Naugatuck to a Georgia electric utility at Macon, the first run-through exercise taking in both N&W and Southern tracks since those systems' 1982 merger as NS. Each 96-car train was to shift just under 10,000 tons of coal a distance of 583 miles. It turned out that although the cars were rapid-discharge hoppers, with which the full

train would be capable of shooting out its entire load in about an hour, without being broken up into individual lots, if the recipient utility had a suitably fitted-out discharge plant, the train was dismantled at destination. (For that matter, it also emerged that the cars were separately loaded in the mine area, so that the operation's "unit train" tag related solely to the fact that it avoided yard-processing en route.) Consequently, each car was taking at least five days over a round trip from the mine to Georgia and back; and its average speed throughout was therefore a dismal 8mph or thereabouts. Comparison with the productivity a trucker would obtain from his machines over the same distance is needless.

If that standard of asset utilization is tolerated with cars that are *not* yard-sorted on the way, then the risk of even worse with the cars that do have to undergo en-route yard reclassification equally needs no stress. One line of attack on this hazard, the concentration of as much reclassification as possible on yards equipped with a battery of computer-based, automated data, and switching systems, is described in the next chapter. Another vital weapon in a freight railroad's armory these days is a computerized operations data system, such as Southern Pacific's TOPS, which keeps a real-time check on the status of all freight cars in use. Taking input from field staff in all traffic originating and receiving centers, and from yards, it records for instant access the loading, unloading (and therefore availability for reassignment), last re-

ported location, and train consist in which it is moving, of each vehicle, together with all pertinent load data. Thus the progress of each and every cargo in transit can be monitored: not only that, but the computer can immediately direct offloaded cars to the most appropriate point offering a new load for that type of vehicle.

With more and more bulk commodity traffic being shoehorned into unit train schemes, a logical concept that would make a train-set completely self-propelled advanced in 1984 from the forlorn standing of one particular US prophet's annual cries in the wilderness to a positive move by the Association of American Railroads to create a prototype. It is known as the integral train.

An integral train would have no separate locomotive. It would be a permanently coupled and probably articulated rake of freight cars, in which

each end vehicle would have a fully-equipped driving cab pure and simple. Traction power plant would be spread throughout the consist. At as many intervals within the consist as gross trainweight made desirable, a diesel engine-generator set would occupy a car frame, feeding its current through underfloor power lines to traction motors fitted to a suitable and widely dispersed portion of the train-set's axles.

The benefits claimed for the integral train theory are enticing. The spread of power, it is argued, would secure improved fuel consumption and payload because it would reduce the dead weight added to a train by a conventional locomotive of comparable output. Permanent coupling of every vehicle would eliminate most problems of controlling coupler slack in an orthodox train, thereby minimizing wear and tear of vehicle structures and derailment risks. If the concept were applied to intermodal merchandise traffic, as it certainly could be, given the rising proportion of dedicated trains run in that sector, this consist stability would also reduce damage to valuable freight

Far left: The traditional caboose, here tailing a Santa Fe unit coal train, is being progressively eliminated with labor union agreement.
Above: The electronic substitute for the caboose: one of several end-of-train brake pressure monitors now marketed is the Trail Guard by Union Switch & Signal.
Right: New intermodal ideas: corn syrup is unloaded from a rail tanker into a road tanker of Chessie System's trucking subsidiary, CMX, for local delivery.

in transit. The integral train's sponsors believe furthermore that it could chop 35 percent off current costs of bulk commodity unit train working and as much as 50 percent of the average bill for operating dedicated intermodal trains, in the latter case in addition to promising more reliable and more transit-time-competitive service, because of its one-piece characteristic. The idea makes still more sense in the mega-merger era, with its enlarged scope for run-through trains and fewer interchange frontiers between railroads.

The AAR was hopeful of having a prototype integral train to test before 1985 was out – but not at its own unrelieved expense. That was where its hope might be dashed. In late 1984

there was little sign that US freight car-builders, at last seeing a little light at the end of the gloomiest tunnel of order deprivation they had ever traveled, were moved by the AAR's enthusiasm to expend their recession-dry bed resources in detailed design and construction of hardware which no railroad had yet shown any indication to order in series.

Before moving on to detailed consideration of the piggyback aspect of intermodal business in the next chapter, one must not overlook the enterprising marriage of road transport to some kinds of orthodox freight car service. Conrail, for example, has developed a flourishing system it calls Flexi-Flo for service of 15 terminals in the Northeast and Midwest. This is for liquid and dry bulk commodities, which the terminals are equipped to transfer speedily from tank to truck with pneumatic and hydraulic pumps. Worth mention, too, is Illinois Central Gulf's Truck-Rail-Truck scheme for door-to-door or port-to-door delivery of finished or semi-

finished steel products, which are loaded on to special pallets (and, particularly in the case of moisture- and damage-sensitive strip coil, protected by plastic shrink wrap) for ease of transfer between rail and highway vehicles.

Finally, one long-lived characteristic of the North American freight train – the tail-end caboose – is now on the way out, for a further cost saving. In 1982 management and labor unions came to a national agreement for phased withdrawal. Each caboose-off proposal had to be separately negotiated under the terms of the pact, and submitted to arbitration if it met dissent. By 1986, 31% of train miles were being run without a caboose. The substitute for the caboose, clamped to a train's rear coupler, is a combination flashing red marker light and electronic device. The latter monitors train-line brake pressure and radio-transmits its readings to a display and control console in the engineer's cab.

4

THE PIGGYBACK BOOM — HOW FAR WILL IT GO?

North American freight railroading took on a new dimension in 1953. The basic principle, granted, was old-hat. As early as the 1850s railroads were ferrying farm waggons and the vehicles of itinerant circuses. Came the internal combustion engine and in the 1930s a few railroads toyed with improvised systems for over-the-rail movement of trucks. It took the rapid post-World War II upsurge of the tractor-and-trailer road rig to rouse the rail industry in general to the potential of custom-built equipment for trunk-hauling road freight transport.

Exploiting the operational flexibility of the unmotored trailer — be it a self-wheeled box or a flat carrying a container — the US trucking industry more than tripled its annual ton-mileage in the first postwar decade and a half. Almost all its new business was high-rated merchandise. That left the railroads heading for dangerously increased dependence, financially, on low-rated bulk commodity freight such as coal and minerals which yielded a comparative pittance per carload. The traditional rail box car was a hopeless contender for much of the road trailer traffic. Often there was no track to get it right to the traffic's source or destination, so that use of rail incurred trans-shipment; the transit time penalty that cost — let alone the extra expense and risk to the cargo — was aggravated by yard processing en route, while the truck headed straight from door to door; and frequently the goods were more economically loaded in a trailer than in a standard boxcar.

However with their ability to trunk-haul up to 10,000 tons with just one train-crew there was the possibility that the railroads could take the trailers off the truckers' hands and move them in trainloads between main centers at less cost than if the trailers were hitched to individually-crewed tractors. The 1953 stimulus to take a serious look at this concept came initially not from a railroad but from General Motors, whose Electromotive Division in that year turned out a purpose-built 75ft flatcar prototype capable of accommodating the standard road trailers of the period. The source of the initiative was not all that surprising. After all, GM had a vested interest in both modes: intermodal development would no way diminish its truck sales, but steady erosion of the rail's merchandise market share could well trim the demand for new diesel locomotives.

Sponsorship as prestigious as GM's guaranteed immediate interest. By the end of 1953 Southern Pacific had decisively adopted the new technique, soon tagged as piggyback, though PR men searched desperately for a more impressive name; and not long afterward the Pennsylvania became a front-runner in the new system. From then on the takeoff was spectacular.

At the close of 1954, 18 railroads were into piggyback, a year later 32 and by 1958, 42. As early as 1955 the piggybacking system together recorded a total of 168,150 carloadings; the gross for 1958 was 276,767; and by 1959 it had soared to 415,156 (the number of trailers moved was, of course, substantially higher, because at least a third of the flatcars involved were each bearing two trailers). Chief protagonists in the 1959 performance were the Pennsylvania, which logged almost 80,000 trailer movements, and Southern Pacific, with some 70,000.

Right: SP mixed COFC/TOFC train swings south over the Sacramento River at Redding, California.

The Pennsylvania was a prime mover in the 1956 establishment of a company, Trailer Train, the concept of which helped significantly to speed the growth of piggyback. Capitalized by the railroads, Trailer Train, or TTX, built up a fleet of purpose-built piggyback for lease to its shareholding railroads, and which they could then run to destinations beyond their own borders free of most of the bureaucratic regulations normally applied to freight cars which were interlined. Thus TTX flats could be reloaded wherever they were discharged, and were trundled about empty much less than the average US freight car.

Today Trailer Train's stock is owned by 17 railroads, and by three non-railroad concerns. It leases other types of flatcar, as well as auto-carriers (or auto-racks), and has subsidiary companies dealing in boxcars and gondolas, but its biggest stock item by far is still the intermodal flat. In 1988 it was deploying no fewer than 46,500 of them. One should add that nowadays many railroads have their own large fleets of intermodal flats; and that vehicles of this kind are also available from several other major freight car leasing companies.

From the start piggyback service has come in five different types, or Plans. Plan I is the "if-you-can't-lick-'em-join-'em" approach to common carrier trucking firms. It offers them just the rail haul of trailers between railroad piggyback terminals – or ramps as they

Above: Santa Fe is experimenting with TOFC tank trailers for both hazardous and non-hazardous products.
Below: The modern successor to yesterday's passenger Limited: an SP TOFC train winds through northern California.

are commonly called, because the circus waggons of earlier years were end-loaded up ramps on to the railroad flats of those days; nowadays top-lifting of trailers from ground to flatcar by crane is generally preferred. Under Plan I the railroad has nothing to do with collection of a trailer from its consignor or with final road delivery; and as a result, of course, it has no contact with the real shipper of the goods.

ICC regulation still tightly limited freedom of both railroad and highway freight operation at piggyback's birth. In 1953 the ICC conceded that though a railroad had no authority to run a trucking service over the highway between a pair of cities, it was at liberty in certain conditions to offer a door-to-door road-rail piggyback-road operation. That encouraged some railroads to

develop their own piggyback-based trucking enterprises and spawn Plan II, for intermodal service at an inclusive rate conducted entirely with railroad equipment; highway trailers as well as flatcars.

The advantage of Plan II to a railroad is naturally personal contact with the customer, plus total control of the operation. The drawback is the need to master the practicalities and economics of a second transportation system. In the early days recourse to Plan II service was also inhibited by the strict regulatory circumscription of the areas at each end of the rail haul in which a railroad could ply its road vehicles, and hence the limited number of sources and destinations for which it could offer Plan II. This constraint vanished with the deregulation of the 1980s.

Plan III is a ramp-to-ramp-only offer like Plan I, but directed at shippers or firms operating their own road vehicles. It gets the railroads back into the movement of merchandise in small lots that would never be tempted into a boxcar, since its main takers are the freight forwarders who bulk such traffic into viable long-haul trailer-loads. Plan IV's prime difference from Plan III is that the shipper is required to own or lease his own flatcars as well as produce the trailers, while Plan V covers a partnership between railroad and common carrier trucker to put on widespread door-to-door service at a jointly-agreed inclusive tariff. Before deregulation the value of Plan V was naturally its scope for a railroad, via its trucking partner, to penetrate areas from which any road transport of its own was debarred – and in so doing to raid other railroads' piggyback business, of course.

During the 1960s and early 1970s piggyback traffic grew steadily, though from time to time the upward curve flattened. But since then, first, the oil price explosion and, second, the dereg-

ulation which has widened the scope for intermodal operation and allowed the railroads to negotiate private, term-based contracts for continuous flows of traffic, expansion has been dynamic.

In 1983 US railroads recorded 2.3 million piggyback carloadings, 400,000 more than in the previous year but over five times the figure at the end of the 1950s – and an even greater advance in terms of trailers piggybacked, since the majority of flats now load a couple of trailers. One railroad alone, Conrail, shifted almost twice as many trailers as the national rail total in 1959. Another, Santa Fe, was making 25 percent of its revenue from piggyback and expected the proportion to reach 50 percent by the century's end. Of all freight carloadings in 1983, 12.4 percent were piggyback; only coal claimed a higher percentage.

These days dedicated piggyback trains – that is, trains carrying exclusively intermodal traffic and running intact between main centers (Union Pacific handles its intermodal business no other way) – are the aristocrats of railroad service on many systems, where they have taken on the aura of

yesteryear's passenger streamliners. One or two have appropriated past streamliner names, in fact: and with justification, considering how smartly they are scheduled.

A case in point is the "Orange Blossom Special." That was once the title of a crack Seaboard Railway streamliner for northeastern cities to the Florida resorts. In 1982 it was revived by CSX for a dedicated piggyback train that exploited that corporation's single-line integration of Seaboard, Richmond, Fredericksburg & Potomac and Chessie System (ex-Baltimore & Ohio) as a through route from Florida to the northeast, and also deregulation, to mount an attack on the fresh produce market surrendered to door-to-door trucking in the 1960s, partly because the railroads' competitive tactics were restrained by regulatory fetters, but not least because of the rigmaroles entailed in interlining the traffic through to the northeast.

This is a Plan II exercise. CSX railroads are firm believers in a one-on-one relationship with their intermodal clients – in other words, in controlling and retailing a complete door-to-door

Right: The two arms of Chessie intermodal-railroad and trucking subsidiary, CMX.

package. So the "Orange Blossom Special" traffic moves in rail-owned trailers which are road-hauled from the growers by the corporation's trucking subsidiary, Chessie Motor Express (CMX), to the train's starting point at Taft Yard, Orlando, on a Florida coast branch from the Seaboard main at Wildwood. The rail flatcars are leased from Trailer Train.

From Orlando to the train's terminal yard at Wilmington, Delaware, is 1,045 miles, taking the Seaboard as far as Richmond, Virginia; the Richmond, Fredericksburg & Potomac from there to Washington, DC; and former Baltimore & Ohio, now Chessie System tracks for the last leg. Yet final road delivery of the produce to northeastern customers, again by CMX, is often achieved within 24 hours of the "Special's" dispatch from Orlando.

Perishables have been one of the key traffics regained by rail since the deregulation of intermodal operation by the ICC in March, 1981. Between then and the end of 1983 Santa Fe, in particular, quickly boosted its annual piggyback hauls of California produce to the east from about 12,000 to over 36,000 trailer-loads. In this case the trailers – 5,000 are dedicated to the operation – are shipper-owned: some railroads are not convinced that getting into total transportation is a wise course, and believe they should stick to what they know best, simply wholesaling use of

the railroad's trunk-haul capability to truckers, forwarders or individual manufacturers who can be persuaded that piggyback is an economical component of their door-to-door transits.

Santa Fe is one prime exponent of the wholesaling school of thought; almost 90 percent of its intermodal trade derives from third-party accounts. Another is Conrail, the country's leading piggyback operator, turning in about 16 percent of all intermodal loadings achieved by US railroads in 1983, and each working day running an average of 34 of its dedicated Trail-Van piggyback trains (four of them reserved for US mail) between one or other of its 34 terminals in the northeast and midwest.

Several Class I systems have no trucking subsidiary and rely for trailer collection and delivery on agreements with motor carriers (NS has arrangements with more than 500). But many others, such as CSX, were prompted by the ICC's 1981 exemption of rail-owned intermodal elements from territorial limitation to set up their own trucking auxiliaries, or else to establish closer liaison with highway subsidiaries already existing within the corporation of which they formed part. Norfolk Southern paid $315 million to buy up North American Van Lines in 1984. Some of these railroad-associated trucking concerns now have authority to operate throughout 48 states: Union

Pacific Freight Services is one, PMT System, part of Southern Pacific Transportation, another.

Another vitally important benefit of deregulation has been freedom to contract for backloads. At the end of the 1970s 61 percent of the trailers which Santa Fe sent east with California produce came back empty, but by 1981's end the ratio had been slashed to 22 percent. Now every one returns with a revenue-earning load.

So what is the outlook for piggyback? The nagging worry is that the profit on piggyback is much too slim for comfort. In the early 1980s that was partly due to the recession's creation of excess freight transportation generally, and the fierce – often quite uneconomic – price-cutting by motor carriers in particular which the railroads had to emulate. Culpable, too, were some railroads which lazily exploited deregulation to undercut neighboring systems for traffic already on rail, instead of getting a marketing act together and prospecting for new business off the highways. But other disturbing factors in piggyback's profitability will not disappear along with the recession or with further easing of fuel prices.

At the outset of the 1980s, when oil prices peaked relative to other costs, rail lobbyists were making much of the fuel-cost savings when trailers were piggybacked in trainload with three or four diesel units up front, instead of

Above left: Seaboard's "Orange Blossom Special" is loaded at Orlando, Florida.

Above: Close-up of traditional TOFC flatcars in the service of a Santa Fe intermodal train.

Above right: Sante Fe TOFC train in desert territory.

individually trunked by highway tractors. But the impact of that contract is steadily diminishing as the gulf widens between rail and road in other sectors of the transportation cost, nowhere more so than in the wages bill.

In 1983 one respected US business analyst computed that on average each mile run by freight train with a crew of standard size incurred labor costs of $12.41, including an allowance for terminal work in putting it together at one end of the run and dismantling it for deliveries at the other. The comparable cost to the truck owner-operator for each mile run by one of his trailers ran at an average of 20 cents. In ten years the ratio had almost doubled in the highway operator's favor. In 1984 it was set to move much further in his direction if the railroad labor unions won anything like the terms they were tabling for their next wage agreements with railroad managements, the more so because the wage-rate outlook in the trucking industry was comparatively stable.

Round about the time that the analysis of road-rail labor costs just outlined was published, Burlington Northern disclosed research of its own which indicated that, with total piggyback operating costs standing where they did in 1983, it was down to mere break-even point at the 700-mile transit mark (which, incidentally, would make all but a fistful of international piggyback routes in Europe financially untenable). If piggyback growth is to continue to be explosive, the railroads have got to dig into the 500-1,000-mile transportation market; there the piggyback potential is infinitely greater than in the 1,000 miles-plus range where rail has made almost all its killings so far. In 1983 BN clearly turned precious few dollars even from the upper end of the shorter-haul trade.

On the other hand it reckoned that by heavy investment in rationalizing and modernizing its piggyback terminals, and in more efficient rail vehicles, coupled with a marketing drive to eliminate empty trailer back-hauls, it could drop the break-even point to at least 550 miles. That would allow it to bid successfully – and economically – for a great deal of new piggyback traffic. But BN also calculated that if the railroad labor unions won all that they were asking for, and rigidly resisted any fresh relaxation of their work rules, the gains from piggyback investment would be completely wiped

out by labor cost escalation. All of which explains why some railroad executives are cautious about plowing more huge sums into development of their intermodal services.

Here and there, one must quickly note, railroads have secured crewing concessions that would make a challenge for shorter-haul traffic worthwhile. With Federal Railroad Administration sponsorship and start-up money, the Milwaukee Road launched one of the best-known, its "Sprint" service over the 410 miles between Chicago and the Twin Cities, Minneapolis and St Paul, operated as a shuttle with fixed formations of flatcars, each innocent of a tail-end caboose, and each making a round trip within 24 hours. For a time the Milwaukee was running six "Sprint" services a day, but the frequency was subsequently reduced. Another pioneer operation of this kind was Illinois Central Gulf's "Slingshot" over the 298 miles between Chicago and St Louis, for which the unions waived the otherwise mandatory two crew changes during the run and agreed to a halved train crew.

The marketing of the "Orange Blossom Special," discussed earlier, was facilitated by Seaboard labor union agreement to exempt the train from three of the five crew changes customary within the mileage traveled by the train in Seaboard territory. The union

also accepted that the "Special" needed only a conductor and a trainman in addition to its cab crew. Boston & Maine and Central Vermont have been able to test the Boston-Montreal market with a "Rocket" overnight piggyback train of only 15 cars, thanks to union consent to its operation with just a two-man crew and no caboose; a similar service has been opened up between Bangor, Maine, and New Haven.

But even so none of the shorter-haul exercises enumerated – excluding the "Orange Blossom Special," that is – has yet turned in a satisfying profit. Other attacks on the cost of piggybacking are essential for continued expansion.

An obvious target is the excessive dead weight in a trailer-piggyback train's gross tonnage. That comes from the need to haul the trailer's idle undercarriage, braking system and the other essentials that make it a highway runner over the rails, as well as those of the rail vehicle carrying it.

One simple solution to that problem already exists: the container (or alternatively a demountable truck or trailer body, commonly called a "swap-body"). Containers already figure in the North American piggyback business, but the

Left: Seaboard System's "Orange Blossom Special" unit TOFC train en route from Orlando, Florida, to Wilmington, Delaware.

Below: First double-stacked container APL Linertrain on UP near Rock Springs, Wyoming.

extent is difficult to define because neither railroads nor the Association of American Railroads segregate container and trailer elements of overall piggyback carloading statistics. In Europe the two kinds of intermodal operation are quite distinct from each other, and managed, marketed and accounted by different subsidiaries within each railroad, though as in the US some railways combine container and trailer loads in the same dedicated intermodal trains.

What is certain is that COFC (Container-on-Flatcar), though it is still hugely overshadowed in volume by TOFC (Trailer-on-Flatcar), is expanding at least as fast and perhaps more rapidly. The dominant element, so far as US railroads are concerned, is maritime containers in import/export traffic. Since the start of the 1980s Soo Line, for one, has more than trebled its maritime container carloadings, with its capture of CP Line and Dart Line traffic between the Canadian border and its Chicago intermodal terminal, which is appealingly located closer to the city's O'Hare airport.

The most striking COFC development of the 1980s, however, has been on the transcontinental routes. A shipping major in Far Eastern trade, American President Lines, is convinced that land-bridging containers of imports by rail from its customary West Coast ports is the economical way to cater for eastern seaboard destinations as well as those in the Midwest, as opposed to shipping the whole way via the Pana-

ma Canal. It owns its own flatcars, which it contracts the railroads to operate in exclusive APL "Linertrains" from the west coast to the transshipment terminals it has installed in ten US cities alongside railroad establishments.

Taking astute advantage of deregulation, APL and the three railroads concerned in Linertrain haulage to the east coast – Union Pacific, Seattle to Fremont (Nebraska); Chicago & North Western, Fremont to Chicago; and Conrail, Chicago to New Jersey – have contrived an ingenious deal with a freight forwarder bulking eastern manufactured goods for the Seattle and San Francisco Bay areas that secures a two-way traffic in the APL containers. Their Far Eastern imports discharged at South Kearny, New Jersey, on the fifth morning after despatch from Los Angeles (the three railroads have hustled a Linertrain of 50 cars and 100 containers the 3,166 miles involved in as little as 79 hours 36 minutes, for an average throughput of 39.8mph inclusive of stops for crew, locomotive changes and so on), the APL containers are promptly reloaded by Transway. The only empty container working occurs, inevitably, when the Transway cargoes are unloaded in the west and the containers are then reassembled at Los Angeles to await the next APL ship. Up to four APL Linertrains are on the move simultaneously, each one completing a round west-east coast trip within a week.

APL maritime containers are also ferried from Los Angeles to Chicago (and back with Transway cargo) over Southern Pacific and Burlington Northern iron. Here, in 1983, APL began wider-scale trial of a Southern Pacific innovation to enhance COFC economics. SP, with its service of several Pacific and Gulf Coast ports, is another railroad with a substantial COFC component in its intermodal trade. At the start of the 1980s it took over from Sea-Land, a major container shipping line, the concept of a low-slung, well-bodied rail vehicle on which containers could be stacked two-high without infringing rail clearances (ex-

cept in some areas of the east, where the restrictive loading gauge still irritatingly limits the scope even of orthodox TOFC operation; the "Orange Blossom Special," for example, has to employ low-platform flats to clear some tunnels in the Washington, DC area). Sea-Land was content with its inspiration; it was reluctant to get embroiled in detailed design and manufacture, hence SP's assumption of the project, which materialized as an articulated unit of five well-bodied carriers, each capable of loading two standard 40ft-long ISO containers. In 1981 SP put 42 of these five-car double-stackers into Los Angeles-Houston service.

In 1983 experiments began with a 20-unit, 200 container-capacity train of double-stackers on the APL Los Angeles-Chicago run, the first transcontinental exploitation of the concept. One of those 20 units was not an SP original, but a prototype – one of the

Above left: SP's version of the double-stack COFC concept in a train heading west through the Arizona desert.

Below: Close-up of SP double-stack COFC cars loading at Los Angeles.

many recently turned out by the railway industry offering more economical COFC/TOFC performance: but of their detail, more shortly – which not only permitted stacking one of the 45ft-long containers now favored by APL atop a 40ft, but thanks to trimming of its tare five-platform weight to only 30 tons scored a 66 percent improvement, no less, in payload/empty vehicle weight ratio over a traditional, single flatcar carrying a brace of 40ft containers.

However, it was in its Seattle-Washington-Kearny (New Jersey) service over UP, CNW, and Conrail that APL began scheduled double-stacked COFC service in July 1984 with a 20-unit train of the Budd-designed Lo-Pac 2000. This is a low-slung, well-body articulated into a five-platform unit, of which each platform averages only 15 tons in tare weight, around 60 percent less than a conventional piggyback flatcar. A double-stacked Lo-Pac 2000 demands a vertical clearance of 19ft 4in, but Conrail overcame that problem by routing the train over its Southern Tier line from Buffalo (NY) to northern New Jersey, which could accommodate the double-stacking after some modest clearance enlargement near Erie (Pennsylvania) and in North Jersey.

Containerization never caught on as a medium for domestic freight movement in the first two decades of North American intermodal transport. In the home arena its use is still comparatively insignificant, but most railroads concede that interest in it is quickening. As yet there are only two which believe that, because of TOFC's inescapable dead weight and therefore cost penalties already outlined, as well as other reasons such as ease of storage, the container must eventually supplant the trailer in the domestic piggyback market.

The most bullish on this point is Canadian Pacific, which has backed its conviction with a heavy investment in domestic container equipment and insists that its COFC has already outstripped its TOFC trade. To swing the balance so sharply against the con-

tinental trend, however, CP Rail had to rethink the container.

Rejecting the modular dimensional standards applied to the vast majority of containers in worldwide trade (though in recent years there has been an increasing tendency to break away from the original ISO formulae, as in the APL 48ft-long boxes just mentioned), CP Rail designed a 44ft 3in-long container with a cross-sectional area bigger than the norm, so that the whole cube resembled as closely as possible the loading space of a highway trailer. Two of them could be loaded on to matching, specially-built 89ft-platform flatcars without their top corners brushing tight loading-gauge clearances. To these big boxes CP Rail has subsequently added a line in 29ft 5in-long containers, three of which can be packed on to one 89ft platform flatcar, with an ingenious bonus for back-loading flexibility: roof hatches and a removable bag liner, so that a contain-

Above: Well-body Lo-Pac 2000, now mass-produced by Thrall for double-stack COFC operation.

er can be loaded one way with a bulk powder, have its bag liner removed after pressure discharge of the powder, and be perfectly fit to accept any merchandise on its next trip. The switch to containers has also helped CP Rail to balance its transcontinental traffic; the vast majority of westbound 44ft-3in boxes return from Vancouver loaded with shipborne merchandise. It claims that its COFC trains are 30 percent more fuel-efficient than TOFC.

Santa Fe, the other advocate of future container supremacy, has also redesigned the container. With Santa Fe's concept we have to consider in detail one of the principal contempor-

Below: CP Rail's outsize 44ft 3in container for domestic traffic.

ary approaches to COFC/TOFC cost-cutting: the conception of a new generation of rail carriers that will both reduce empty vehicle weight and pack containers or trailers into smoother aerodynamic shape as a trainload. The two improvements together are calculated to lower substantially the amount of traction and fuel needed to rail-haul any given COFC/TOFC train payload.

Santa Fe was the first railroad to get one of these new-generation rail-carriers into fleet use. The design, which was its own and which it first called the "Ten-Pack" but later and more evocatively the "Fuel-Foiler," set a pattern which has been followed by many of the numerous supply firms that have since bid for what could be a massive reinvestment market with their own prototype hardware.

The "Ten-Pack" articulates ten platforms – that is, adjoining platforms are carried on a single linking truck. Each platform is little more than a strong, skeletal center sill to bear a single trailer, with short aprons extended each side of the sill at one end to support the trailer's highway wheels. This stripped-to-essentials approach makes a loaded "Ten-Pack" 35 percent lighter than the gross of ten highway trailers carried on five traditional TOFC flatcars. Moreover, on a "Ten-Pack" the trailers are packed closer to each other and nearer ground level, for better aerodynamic outline.

Initially Santa Fe employed its "Ten-Packs" purely for TOFC, running them in 10-unit and thus 100-trailer capacity train-sets on its dedicated TOFC service between Los Angeles and Chicago. Straight away it found it was saving 5,500 gallons of diesel fuel on each round trip of some 4,400 miles, or in cash terms well over $4,000 a time.

Then Santa Fe created its own version of a container which could be double-stacked on a "Ten-Pack" platform, though in 1987 it was still at the stage of physically proving and test-marketing half-a-dozen prototypes (three made of fiberglass, three of aluminum) and had yet to set up a produc-

Above right: A train of Santa Fe's "Fuel Foiler" lightweight TOFC cars is loaded.
Above: Deep-sea COFC business for Canadian National at Halifax, Nova Scotia.
Below: Transcontinental TOFC train of Santa Fe's "Fuel Foiler" near Victorville, California, bound for Chicago.

Facing page, above left: Standard forklift trucks can enter a "Fuel Foiler" container to load palletised traffic.
Facing page, center: "Fuel Foiler" containers can load grain.
Facing page, bottom: Santa Fe's "Fuel Foiler" container.
Facing page, above right: Double-stacking of "Fuel Foiler" containers.

tion line for this "Fuel Foiler" container. The 45ft-long container is broadly A-shaped, with outside, continuous legs that straddle the center platform of a "Ten-Pack," and its roof has a broad ridge which fits snugly between the legs of another "Fuel Foiler" container stacked on top of it. That ridge creates headroom for a forklift to operate right inside the container for loading or discharge of palletized merchandise in particular, but the container also has all the fittings for use in bulk commodity traffics, such as grain, powders – or even coal. Needless to say, because of its unusual shape as well as its high cubic size, Santa Fe have had to develop a special highway chassis for it.

Mention of the "Fuel Foiler" container's length is a reminder that expanding trailer lengths have injected one more complication into TOFC development. Trailer Train has already had to modify almost a third of its 49,500 intermodal flatcars so that each can squeeze on a pair of the 45ft-long highway trailers which in the early 1980s were fast superseding 40ft-long vehicles. Many railroads with their own flatcar fleets were busy with similar conversions, though the 45ft trailer was not expected to dominate intermodal loads until the end of the decade.

But 45ft is not the end of the story. The Surface Transportation Assistance Act of 1982 legalized nationwide a 48ft trailer length (or haulage of two 28ft trailers), and with body width expanded from 96 to 102in; tandem 28ft-

trailer operation had begun before 1983 was out, in fact. New rail equipment design has had to take account of this important variable.

There are also many other variables. Should future cars be designed specifically for either COFC or TOFC, or be contrived to suit either type of intermodal traffic? While articulation of cars over a single truck is an undeniably sensible way of saving weight, is the resultant risk of having a multiplatform unit unserviceable because of a defect in just one platform worth taking? Is it wiser to save weight by fitting independent or semi-independent platforms with single-axle trucks (bearing in mind that the Europeans have perfected two-axle freight cars capable of perfectly smooth and safe operation at 75mph)? What is the ideal number of platforms to build into an articulated right for normal traffic demand and operating convenience – three, five or more up to ten, as in the Santa Fe model? Is the low-slung well-body preferable to a skeletal frame?

By mid-1984 one was losing count of the number of manufacturers, enticed by the potentially massive market opening up for a new generation of intermodal cars if TOFC growth and general economic revival are not checked, which had invested their own resources in prototype responses to these

Above: Southern Pacific was first to operate lightweight new-generation "Impack" TOFC cars in full trains. These are loading SP "Golden Pig" trailers at Oakland, California.
Below: Prototype single-axle-truck TOFC flatcars by Pullman-Standard.

Above: Close-up of "Impack" skeletal flatcar in SP service.

Bottom: Prototype articulated COFC four-unit car by Berwick Forge & Fabricating.

questions. In sum, these prototypes offered the railroad industry a chance to test practically each option summarized in the previous paragraph, and others besides.

For reasons discussed earlier, the majority of railroads were not hurrying to their order books. A number were happy for the time being to limit their capital expenditure and meet rising piggyback demand and increasingly resort to longer trailers by comparatively inexpensive flatcar conversions from their huge stocks of idle boxcars. Norfolk Southern, for instance, while it was buying some new flatcars, was breaking down 1,000 boxcars into intermodal flats in its own workshops for just $8.4 million.

By early summer 1984, nevertheless, more than 2,500 of the new lightweight piggyback platforms were operational. At that juncture Burlington Northern, Santa Fe, and Southern Pacific were the only railroads to have infused the new models into their own fleets, and generally in no more than sample quantities. Elsewhere, as just described, APL has invested in 65 five-platform units of the Budd Lo-Pac 2000 design.

The intriguing question was whether Trailer Train's innovative choice for the first phase of its fleet rebuilding with new-generation platforms would influence other buyers. By the fall of 1984 the company had laid orders for 700 of Thrall Car's 11-ton "Front Runner," a platform long enough to take a 50ft highway trailer, yet mounted on two-axle trucks of European design, supplied by Krupp of West Germany. Trailer Train predicted that this single-platform design would form 80 percent of its renewals, because of its operational flexibility, and articulated five-platform units the residual 20 percent.

Above right: Close-up of a single-axle truck in Trailer Train's lightweight "4-Runner" TOFC flatcar.

Right: The scale of today's intermodal traffic: Santa Fe's Cornwith Yard, Chicago.

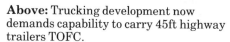

The growing role of the container has added impetus to another critically important cost-cutting drive, the paring down of piggyback terminals to a limited number, strategically sited to cater for all worthwhile traffic sources by easy road collection and delivery, and, because of their smaller number but individual high-volume through-put, justifying a high degree of mechanized handling. In the early 1970s US railroads together were offering piggy-back service from some 1,300 terminals. In the spring of 1984 the total was already down to little more than 400; and still contracting. The more the number of terminals drops, of course, the greater is the inducement to concentrate the massed traffic between them into dedicated COFC/TOFC trains that are immune from yard remarshaling en route and thus to the protracted, unreliable transits of cargoes which in the past have contrasted so bleakly with the assurance of door-to-door, over-the-highway trailer haulage.

The in-word for a rail intermodal terminal these days in "hub-center." "Circus ramp" is out. Hub-center signifies not only a terminal catering for the whole of a high-volume hinterland, but one furnished for exclusive top-lift road-rail transshipment of trailers or container – increasingly, both – by mobile gantry or side-loading crane. Incidentally, the mechanical handling industry has responded to the piggy-back boom with a range of ever-more-versatile cranage prototypes just as profuse as the vehicle industry's output of lightweight piggyback platform cars. By mid-1984 almost half the US rail-roads' piggyback terminals were effectively mechanized hub-centers.

The latest, newly-built or remodeled hub-center is generally long and lean in shape, and one or more of its tracks is open-ended or run-through, not a dead-

Above: Trucking development now demands capability to carry 45ft highway trailers TOFC.

end siding. That minimizes switching and consequently saves some operating cost. Tracks are long enough for a full train to be assembled on a single road, its cars ready-blocked for the different destinations it serves, so that it is ready to move off as soon as its line-haul locomotives have backed on. Union Pacific's Los Angeles terminal has only four tracks, but together they have room to place 200 piggyback platforms each of 89ft length; in contrast, Santa Fe's Chicago terminal, sprawling over four times as much acreage, has 11 tracks but standing room for only 209 platforms.

Dispense with all need of intermodal transshipment – in other words, devise an 'amphibian' vehicle that can use both rail track and highway – and then, of course, you have at least in theory a way of reducing the terminal costs. Back in the 1960s two Chesapeake & Ohio engineers came up with just such an invention, the RoadRailer. It was essentially a road trailer, but with interchangeable, individually retract-able rail and tired highway wheel assemblies at its rear end, each with appropriate suspension and braking systems. To change from one mode to

Left: Santa Fe is one railroad which expects COFC eventually to outpace TOFC.

another, the only terminal requirement was an air line to power the rearwheel assemblies' changeover mechanism and a hard standing around the rails to carry the highway wheels when they were in play. In the rail mode, the trailer's front end interlocked with the rear of its neighbor to create a firm coupling and air connections for Road-Railer train formation. A special adaptor vehicle was needed to make a coupling bridge between a locomotive's conventional fittings and the lead vehicle of the RoadRailer train.

The RoadRailer had some limited C&O employment in the 1960s but no other railroad took it up and before long it disappeared. That was partly attributable to conservatism, but just as much to the high initial cost of the RoadRailer on the one hand, and its meager payload capacity compared with that of a standard road trailer pure and simple.

The last objection has been muted since the idea was resurrected and redeveloped by Bi-Modal Corporation, a company under the wing of a major in the wagon-building and leasing business, Tiger International, at the end of the 1970s. In its latest incarnation the RoadRailer, in its box trailer version, is offered in either 45 or 48ft body lengths, and able to load up to 48,000lb of freight without its duplicated wheel-braking assemblies infringing highway axle-load limits. It is available, moreover, as a refrigerated box, an auto-carrier, a COFC flat and as a tank as well as a conventional box trailer.

Throughout the early 1980s the RoadRailer's new sponsors proclaimed with rising confidence that "its time had come." One or two railroad executives allowed that they might just be right. After exhaustive laboratory-condition tests on the then Federal Railroad Administration-managed test track at Pueblo had passed the first redeveloped prototypes as fit for 75-car train operation at standard intermodal train speeds, service tests on railroads in Canada as well as the US confirmed not only that, but adduced that a

RoadRailer train gave freight a smoother ride at 19 percent less operating cost than orthodox TOFC equipment.

However no one bought them. Except for short-lined operation by Illinois Central Gulf of a leased train between Louisville and Memphis, which ICG shut down in October 1982 claiming unsatisfying traffic, Bi-Modal had to live on shoulder-pats for enterprise and soothing reiterations of interest from one or two railroad head offices. Technical reservations were not the reason for this railroad diffidence, but the fact that the RoadRailer was and is incompatible with other intermodal systems: in other words, because RoadRailers cannot be conveniently coupled up to normal COFC/TOFC cars, a RoadRailer service has to be packaged and marketed as a segregated trainload operation.

Eventually that point was taken by Bi-Modal itself. In 1983 commercial RoadRailer service at last took off when a New York forwarder was persuaded to take on 100 refrigerated RoadRailers for a tri-weekly haul of produce from the Orlando-Sebring area of Florida to a New York terminal in the Bronx (inaccessible to orthodox TOFC, by the way, because that would not clear the Hudson River tunnel approach to the city, so that this operation should have boosted the RoadRailer as an eastern seaboard intermodal system); and Bi-Modal itself created a marketing subsidiary to manage to sell a RoadRailer full-train service, the "Empire State Xpress," between Rochester, Buffalo, and New York, which Conrail accepted for operation over its tracks with Conrail locomotives and train-crews.

Soon Burlington Northern, the railroad which had been looking likeliest to translate encouraging noises into positive action, indicated that before 1984 was out it was prepared to run for this Bi-Modal subsidiary a "South West Xpress" over the 1,270 miles between Chicago and Houston, calling intermediately at Kansas City, Tulsa, and Dallas-Fort Worth. It would call for a

Above: A 5-unit RoadRailer train on the Richmond, Fredericksburg & Potomac south of Washington DC during early 1980s trial service.

fleet of about 1,100 RoadRailers, some of them container flats and others 45ft-long "Coolrailers," as the refrigerated box variant had been tagged. Also firmly on the cards, it was said, was a comparable "Pacific Coast Xpress" over Southern Pacific iron between Los Angeles and the San Francisco Bay area.

Maybe the RoadRailer's time was at least in sight, if not yet arrived. But abruptly, in mid-1984, Bi-Modal announced termination of the "Empire State Xpress" operation. The reasons underlined the anxieties over piggyback running costs already outlined. Solid business had been accumulated over the service's 18 months' life; it had never been scathed by a vehicle failure en route; its fuel consumption was half that of an orthodox TOFC train of comparable payload, because the Road-Railer's modest tare weight meant that the 60-vehicle train needed only one 3,000hp locomotive for traction; and the labor unions had assented to its operation without a caboose and with a reduced three-man crew. But the service could not staunch a loss of $100,000 a month. Some blame was laid on Conrail's charges for running the train, plus the fact that crews had to be changed three times in the 425-mile run and that each man drew a premium $40,000-60,000 a year to redress the agreement to a smaller crew.

5
THE COMPUTER AGE IN TRAFFIC CONTROL AND FREIGHT CAR SORTING

Almost 60 years elapsed between the first two seminal developments in the application of electrical power to traffic control and train safety systems. The first, in the early 1870s, was the invention of the track circuit, the passage through running rails of a weak electric current which was short-circuited by the wheels of a passing train, thereby registering the latter's presence. The second, at the close of the 1920s, was the realization that switches and signals could be controlled at a considerable mileage from a dispatching center if they were power-operated. That was the genesis of Centralized Traffic Control (CTC), the concentration of train control over 50 and more miles of route in the hands of a single dispatcher. In a third of the time between those important steps the past two decades' hectic advance in the sciences of electronics, microprocessors, and computers has not only achieved more significant progress already, but also made ultimate control of a whole railroad from one center a credible possibility.

Basically, a railroad main line is still signaled the same way as it was over half-a-century ago. It is divided spatially into so-called blocks: and except in certain strictly safeguarded circumstances, only one train at a time must occupy each block. Signals are sited to secure a safe block's headway between succeeding trains; and the insulation of each track circuit from its neighbors naturally corresponds with the block sectioning.

Track circuiting is a pivotal, multifunction component of modern signaling and traffic control systems. The primary role of a circuit, when it is deenergized by a passing train, is to activate protection of that train, either by closing locks on the controls of switches and signals conflicting with the train's patch, or, on an open stretch of line devoid of switches and junctions, directly setting signals in the train's rear to danger until it has cleared the block and safe headway distance has been established between it and any following train. The latter system, in which trains are effectively signaling themselves, is known as automatic block signaling.

Track circuiting also purveys vital information on the location and progress of individual trains to a CTC dispatcher's desk via a train describer system. The present-day CTC operator sits in front of an illuminated representation of the whole track layout he supervises; it used to be in the form of a fixed panoramic display, but the trend nowadays – of which more shortly – is into reproduction on a series of color video screens, or CRTs. That display shows not only the current status of each route, switch and signal under the operator's control, and not merely which blocks are occupied by trains, but also each train's identity by its working number. When a train enters or starts in the CTC dispatcher's territory, he keys its identity and block section point of origin into the train describer. Then as the train moves from block to block and successive track circuits report the progress to the train describer, that will automatically

Right: The hump layout at Seaboard's Waycross, Georgia, Rice Yard allows two trains to be sorted simultaneously into the classification sidings (at rear).

and accordingly move its identifying number from one berth to the next on the operator's illuminated layout display.

One should add that track circuits are no longer exclusively electrical. Nowadays they are also electronic, transmitting their commands in pulsed codes through the running rails. Solid state circuiting has the advantages of reduced installation time and more proof against weather, deterioration, or even vandalism. Moreover, as today's highly automated urban metros and subways in particular demonstrate, it is now possible to superimpose a range of audio-frequency codes on track circuitry, so as to convey all manner of driving command from a control center to a train's traction, braking, and other equipment in one direction; and to return automatically confirmatory responses and other data to the control center.

Electronics have also revolutionized the extent and complexity of layout which can be feasibly controlled from a single center. In CTC's early days each remotely-operated signal or switch had to have its individual two-wire connection to the CTC dispatcher's panel, one wire to transmit the command, the other to return confirmation of the apparatus' function. Only one piece of apparatus at a time could be addressed from the panel; and it could take five seconds or more to complete the transaction by receipt of response. Obviously that limited the usefulness of CTC in

terms of the traffic density and distance manageable by one command center.

Modern electronics have accelerated speed of transmission and response more than a hundredfold. Furthermore a single wire – or, increasingly nowadays, microwave channel – can accommodate a large number of messages speeding both ways simultaneously. One means of differentiating between the addresses of each message is frequency coding. Another is by use of ultra-high-speed electronic scanners, one at the panel end, one at the remote interlocking end of the channel, each precisely synchronized with each other, so that they simultaneously check each panel control

against its apparatus addressee several times a second for lack of correspondence. As soon as the remote interlocking scanner detects an altered state in a panel control, signifying that it has been reset by the operator, it activates the relevant addressee apparatus to correspond: then, conversely, the panel scanner will note a discrepancy and automatically record on the operator's panel that the addressee apparatus has responded correctly.

Automatic cover for a communication system failure is possible. This is a feature of Southern Pacific's 1983 CTC installation by the Union Switch & Signal Division of American Standard Inc on the Topeka-Herington sector of SP's newly acquired ex-Rock Island Tucumcari-Kansas City line, for example. There a field failure protection device, microprocessor-based, immediately takes over if it detects a communications breakdown and automatically signals the trains safely through their meets until order is res-

Above left: The CTC operator's position in Chessie's computer-based center at Columbus, Ohio.

Below: A typical thumb-switch-operated CTC operator's panel.

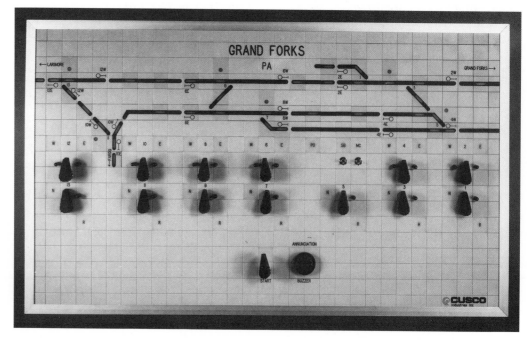

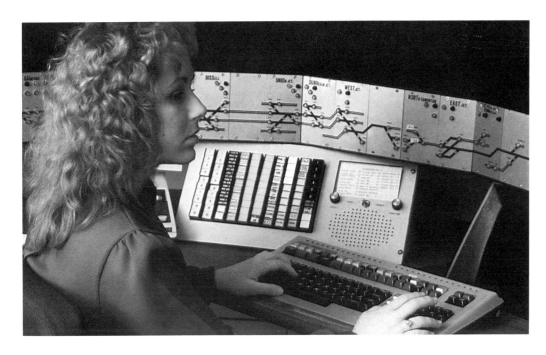

tored. That Topeka-Herington scheme, incidentally, exemplifies the operating economy of CTC: under Rock Island the line was double-track with automatic block signaling, but with its traffic efficiently regulated by modern CTC from a single panel, it has been possible to reduce the 83 miles largely to single line, though its passing loops do range in length up to a substantial 14 miles.

There was one application of computers and microprocessors which US railroads were in the mid-1980s still reluctant to take up, though several European railroads were by then overcoming their reservations. That was direct operation of route-setting switch, and signal movement. Because 'failsafe' is every signal engineer's credo, there is hesitation to abandon use of relays for individual apparatus actuation in response to panel controls, despite the resultant bulk, cost, and intricacy of a major interlocking's relay room. In Europe, however, the Swedes in particular have already proved that resort to computer control does not prejudice safety. Their safeguard is to pass panel controls simultaneously to a pair of parallel-connected computer systems. Each is arranged to examine command and addressee apparatus in a different way, then to double-check the other's findings before a command is passed on to the addressee for action.

But the impact of computers on other elements of traffic control is impressive enough. Consider, for example, the scope of General Railway Signal's (GRS) Micro Traffic Master II system as applied to the computer-aided operations center of Burlington Northern's Springfield Region, which covers at least 1,750 miles of line, including main routes from St Louis to Denison, Texas; Kansas City to Birmingham; St Louis to Memphis; and the busy Kansas City-Denison sector.

There are just four dispatcher workstations in the center. These face a wall-mounted array of 19 color-video (CRT) screens, which together display the track layout of the whole area controlled by the center, the current

status of its individual switches and signals, and the block locations and identities of all trains in the territory, as previously described. (Should a dispatcher forget to key in to the train describer the identity of a train entering the territory or starting within it, the train describer will automatically assign it a unique code which the dispatcher can later correct.)

Each operator has a typewriter-like keyboard, on which he taps out the appropriate codes to set switches and signals, to feed train identities to the train describer, or call up staff in the field. He also has his own CRT on which he can call up a representation of the layout and train occupation status in a part of the territory in more detail. Though it is not employed in this BN installation, GRS also offers the possibility of eliminating the separate keyboard control medium: the dispatcher has just to touch the switch and signal he wants to alter on his CRT display of the layout to initiate a command. Either way the apparatus will record on the CRT the details of the command selected and give the operator a chance to check his selection before the message is transmitted to ground apparatus. The CRT will also indicate an error if the operator has tried to set up a route that the safety interlocking will not allow.

Another important feature of each dispatcher work-station is access to an Operations Reporting System. This automatically generates valuable data

Above: The despatcher's desk of CN computer-based traffic control system at Edmonton.

that once needed laborious manual compilation. Fed with input both from the train describer and the operator's keyboard, it automatically registers all switch and signal movements and the specific train for which they were ordered, and in different ways logs the treatment and progress of each train as it threads the territory. Each work station has an additional black-and-white TV monitor on which its operator can call up data of previous train handling for reference. It is worth adding, incidentally, that there is no rigid partition of territory between each work-station; there are means to reassign territory between stations at will, so that more attention can be paid to locations where traffic is intense while elsewhere activity has temporarily eased off.

The most sophisticated element of the GRS Traffic Master II is its computerized dispatching aids. Once a train entering or starting in his territory has had its identity keyed into the train describer, the operator can leave its routing entirely to the computer, which after checking its memory bank to ascertain the train's schedule and destination will path it through to that destination. Besides performing all necessary switching, it will anticipate problems of passing the train through oncoming traffic on a single line, organize the necessary loop meets and automatically brief the operator, by setting up the data on his desk video monitor on how it has resolved each confrontation. The computer also monitors the progress of trains and predicts their forward arrival and departure times.

The operator has means to override the computer and exercise his own judgement and control at any time. Or he can opt for partial aid from the computer, under what GRS calls the "Green carpet" level of automatic dispatching: in this mode the computer clears the road for just two or three blocks in advance of the train and no more. Whatever level of automation the operator prefers, it will be obvious that these computer aids and the automatic logging and recording devices described earlier eliminate a lot of the manual drudgery from a dispatcher's job. The corollary of that is naturally that fewer dispatchers are needed to oversee a given territory or intensity of traffic.

One could fill much of this book's remaining pages with examples of the many different uses electronic processors now find in rail operations management and traffic control. Apart from application to car processing in classification yards, which will be discussed shortly, just two instances must suffice.

First, Union Pacific's amplification of the functions of a hotbox detector, that all-important trackside device beamed at the running gear of passing trains to sense any overheating of axleboxes – a potentially hazardous condition which can lead to fire or derailment. UP has lately installed on its busy Nebraska main line a series of microprocessor-based detectors equipped with electronic scanners that first of all take due account of ambient conditions, such as whether the sun is out, wind direction, and air temperature, to verify that these in no way distort the temperature readings they are taking from each passing axle. If a detector still spots a risky abnormality, it automatically sets a signal to danger ahead of the affected train.

Simultaneously the detector fires off via UP's microwave communications system two sets of data on the incident, one to UP's faraway Omaha technical laboratories, the other to the territory's dispatching center. At the latter the dispatcher is immediately alerted by an alarm, whereupon a computer starts to disgorge a readout specifying just where the train is in trouble, its speed when the trouble was detected, and the individual temperatures the device recorded for each axle in its consist.

Hot box detectors and other automa-

Above: CN installs signalling in British Columbia.

tic sensors of defects in passing trains, such as dragging brakes or maladjusted wagon loads, can be linked up to visual trackside displays that illuminate warnings to head-end train crews. The latest development, however, is the "talking" detector, the microprocessor of which is connected to a voice synthesizer/transmitter that translates the detector's reading into words and broadcasts a fully detailed warning to

Above: Under CTC control, a westbound Burlington Northern freight emerges from the 7.8-mile Cascade Tunnel in Washington State and enters a passing loop.

Right: The operating desk of BC Rail's Location Identification Control (LIC) system at the North Vancouver center.

the engineer over his cab radio. CP Rail, for one, is now working to supplement this service with a visual reminder of the information for the engineer, through development of ancillary devices that will reproduce the transmitted data in digital form on a cab display panel.

The second application of computers deserving brief description is Burlington Northern's COMPASS system, which has valuably improved BN's efficiency in deployment of its locomotives. This collates information both from BN's main computerized data system and from staff in the field to present the railroad's central operations HQ with advance data on all train consists and tonnage, the routes they will follow and any restrictions those impose on choice of locomotive, plus the current location and status of every locomotive on BN's books. It is all displayed on a bank of color video screens, each of which can show full details of up to 36 train consists at a time, in the operations center.

A computer-based dispatching and operations control system of the range and complexity of GRS' Traffic Master II is extremely costly. It would be an absurd extravagance for many lines carrying only a few trains daily, but on many of the less intensively worked routes effective operations management and monitoring of traffic is just as essential nowadays, both for economy in use of equipment and for commercial credibility.

An excellent example of modern technology's adaptation to this kind of need is the Location Identification Control (LIC) system, devised by Canada's Glenayre Electronics, which is installed on the British Columbia Railway. LIC even dispenses with track circuiting. The presence and position of trains is registered by transponders, passive electronic devices each set to an individual code, which are laid in the track at intervals of about a mile. Each BCR locomotive and railcar is fitted with a receiver that energizes and interrogates each transponder and picks up its unique code, then passes it to an associated microprocessor which thereby registers the train's location on the route. Back at BCR's North Vancouver HQ a computer is continuously scanning the

rail territory, automatically interrogating the equipment of each locomotive and railcar to ascertain its position as established by its last transponder reading. It conducts this inquisition and gets the responses back by radio transmission over the microwave network, which also provides voice communication between control center and train crews. From its record of the times at which a train passes successive transponders, the computer can naturally establish its speed as well as its position.

Another important transponder development taking shape in the early 1980s was a reliable Automatic Car Identification (ACI) system, a vital asset in customer relations since it offers automatic monitoring of an individual freight car's progress throughout its transit from shipper to recipient. In this case it is the transponder which is vehicle-mounted, its unique code representing the individual fleet number of that vehicle. The interrogating device is laid in the track and reads off the transponder code of each car in a train, decodes the data and transmits it automatically to the selected operations control center.

The beauty of the transponder is that it needs no power supply of its own. It is completely inert until the microwave signal targeted on it by the interrogator soaks it with enough energy to rouse it into emitting its code; interrogation and response take only 100 milliseconds at most, generally much less, so that accurate vehicle identifica-

tion throughout a train making as much as 120mph is ensured. The interrogators, incidentally, can be arranged to switch on only when a train is in their vicinity. It is worth remarking, too, that in many remote locations where normal weather conditions allow, more energy costs still are being saved by fitting trackside devices of this and other types described to work off stored solar power.

Keeping tabs on the whereabouts of individual cars on the move is valuable, but the place where they can easily be mislaid or mishandled is the classification yard where line-haul trains are formed or dismantled into car lots for transfer to other trains or local deliveries. The yard is a freight railroad's Achilles heel in its bid for more truckloads of general merchandise freight. As a previous chapter stressed, the railroad offers its most price- and quality-competitive service when it can run a unit train intact from freight source to user without any halt to resort the cars en route. When it is dealing in traffic that moves in less-than-full-trainload lots, a railroad has less scope to maximize its trump card, its supreme economy in hauling huge tonnage over the road in a single train movement, with infinitely less crew than a comparable trucking exercise would demand. Whereas a trucker heads straight from consignor to consignee, the railroad has to process the freight from local train to main-line train, quite likely from one main-line train to another en route, then finally to a local

delivery trip, all at worrying cost not only in cash but in time added to the freight's transit.

The capital cost is enormous, but in the big-city traffic crossroads and gateways of the North American rail system above all, the long-term solution is to reduce the number of classification yards and concentrate train sorting on the smallest practicable number of giant installations equipped with the latest aids to quick and accurate remarshaling of cars. The mega-mergers, of course, have given this process a fillip. When Norfolk & Western and Southern, for example, came together as Norfolk Southern, one of the new corporation's earliest moves was to consolidate yard facilities at the ten most important centers where the two constituent railroads previously bordered each other, such as Cincinnatti, Ohio and East St Louis, Illinois.

Microprocessors and computers are key tools of the modern classification yard. For an impression of their value, consider the huge Queensgate yard which the Chessie System completed at Cincinnatti in 1982, and which is now Chessie's exclusive center in that city for origination of line-haul trains, though five of the other 13 yards which Chessie originally operated in Cincinnatti survive to handle sorting of local industrial traffic.

Queensgate is grand-scale. Three of its reception tracks for incoming trains to be sorted can each hold a consist as long as 225 cars; and three of its six departure tracks that berth sorted trains waiting to pull out can each accommodate a train of up to 185 cars. The classification tracks themselves are arranged to block traffic for as many as 110 different principal des-

Far left: Use of a computer to make up train sets consists at Santa Fe's Hobart Yard, Los Angeles.
Left: Control tower of Southern Pacific's West Colton Yard, Los Angeles.
Right: Part of Santa Fe's huge Barstow Yard. A train is being sorted over the hump (left center) into classification tracks (foreground).

tinations. Commissioning of Queensgate has in fact reduced the number of classification tracks needed in the Cincinnatti terminal area's yards of Chessie System as a whole by almost a third.

Sorting of trains is completely computer-controlled. One computer system, known as the Management Information System (MIS), assimilates the details of an incoming train – the destinations of its cars, their type, loaded weight and so on – well in advance of its arrival at Queensgate from data fed to it by the train's last yard point of origin. Referring this information to the destinations prescribed for each Queensgate classification track by the Yardmaster, MIS has instructions assigning the train's cars to their appropriate classification tracks ready for action when it rolls on to one of the reception tracks.

Queensgate is a hump yard: that is, the reception tracks are separated from the classification tracks by a crested "throat." A train being sorted is propelled over the hump, with its cars already uncoupled as necessary to distribute them to their designated classification tracks, into which they roll by gravity from the crest of the hump. On the classification track side of the hump the switches have to be swiftly reset as necessary between each descending car or "cut" of more than one car, to segregate them to their respective tracks.

Close control of speed is essential as the train to be sorted is propelled over the hump. This can be secured by fitting yard switching locomotives with a rheostatic device that will hold their speed at an unvarying 2.5mph, irrespective of the load they are pushing. Nowadays remote control of

unmanned, robot locomotives from a hump control office is a feasible alternative; it is practised in Europe by the German Federal Railway and in North America is being pioneered by Canadian National in its Symington yard at Winnipeg.

Once humping has begun at Queensgate, the only human function is to monitor the action. As cars roll off the hump, a Process Control (PC) system, having digested the classification track assignment list formulated by the MIS system, automatically resets the switches between "cuts." A sequence of retarders, devices which apply braking pressure to the wheels of descending wagons, automatically retard the wagons by an amount carefully graduated to reflect their type and weight as recorded by the MIS computer system. (The man in charge of the humping operation, incidentally, has a video-screen in his office which gives him an advance sight of cars coming up to the hump's crest: the MIS system alerts him to watch for any car with load of a volume character, or a potentially hazardous cargo, which is desirably not humped the usual way, but individually sorted by a locomotive, so that he can temporarily halt the automation process.) Finally, as the humped cars come quietly to rest in their assigned classification tracks, the MIS system automatically logs the accumulating contents of each road in detail.

Even in a comprehensively modernized classification yard like the Queensgate, the average time that a freight car spends between arrival and departure, duly processed, is still disturbing. Conrail, for example, was happy in 1983 that reequipment of its huge 72-classification track, 2,200-car capacity Elkhart yard in Indiana had clipped the average detention of a car for processing there from 20-21 to 18 hours. But in those 18 hours a railroad freight car was effectively halted on its journey. During the same elapsed time a cargo trucked over the highway would be at least 500 miles nearer its destination.

6
THE RISING EFFICIENCY OF THE AMERICAN DIESEL LOCOMOTIVE

The opening years of the 1980s were the bleakest that North America's big locomotive builders had endured since the dieselization tide swept steam aside. In 1978-80 the industry had filled orders for over 4,400 new locomotives. But the 1981 total was only 522 and in 1982 that slipped to around 400.

At the start of 1983, reduced to an average output of one locomotive a day (compared with 5½ ten years earlier), General Motors' Electro-Motive Division plant at La Grange, Illinois, was employing little more than a fifth of its full production capacity. A year previously GM had had to rebut a report in the Chicago *Tribune* that La Grange would be shut through the 1982 summer because business was so dispiriting. Both in 1983 and 1984, however, Bombardier Inc in Canada was compelled to close for the summer because of meager orders. The outlook was no happier at General Electric's Erie plant in Pennsylvania, where anxieties were heightened by the company's heavy investment in automation of many Erie manufacturing processes or at GM Canada's Diesel Division in London, Ontario.

All this was scarcely surprising, seeing that in January 1983 the Class I railroads had around 5,500 locomotives, or almost a quarter of their total stock, laid up. The prime reason, of course, was severe tonnage downturn as a result of national recession. Allied to that was the preference of several major systems, such as Santa Fe, Southern Pacific, and Union Pacific, for remanufacture of existing units rather than new buys while pinched revenues were being closely pressed by costs.

Rejuvenation of ageing or technically obsolescent units for extended life has been widespread practice for decades past. If the rebuild runs up a bill exceeding the unit's original purchase price by more than 50 percent, then it is accounted a Capital Rebuild and as such qualifies under both ICC and Internal Revenue Service rules for the same investment tax concession as a new buy; and its depreciation can extend over the whole period of its projected new life, which can be as much as 15 years. A Capital Rebuild frequently involves re-engining, often with a later higher-horsepower model – for instance, one from the EMD 645 range in place of an earlier 567 – and generally a complete rewiring and renewal of electrical components. Remanufacture is not without pitfalls; one is difficulty in matching latest-model assemblies with some fitments in older locomotive shells that can be hard or very costly to reshape; another is the ever-decreasing availability of good-quality spares for repair of the retained elements of the original locomotive structures and running gears.

Several railroads remanufacture in their own shops, such as Southern Pacific at Sacramento, California, and Santa Fe at Cleburne, Texas, and San Bernadino, California. Another, Missouri Pacific, completed in the summer of 1984 a $40 million transformation of its North Little Rock, Arkansas, heavy repair and remanufacturing plant into a complex with three times the capacity

Right: Chessie System's Cumberland, Maryland, locomotive shops. Some locomotives are still in former Baltimore & Ohio livery.

Above: A brace of GM-EMD FP40H diesels lead the "Coast Starlight" into Seattle.

Right: Two ex-Louisville & Nashville GM-EMD GP16s and a GE Type U18B front a Seaboard unit boxcar train moving Coors beer in bulk.

of the original, and a claim to fame as the biggest and most sophisticated such enterprise on any US railroad.

But the extent of remanufacturing has also induced private enterprise to get into the business. In 1971 Precision National went into partnership with Illinois Central Gulf to develop locomotive remanufacture at ICG's Paducah, Kentucky, shops into a contract service open to all comers. Two years later Morrison-Knudsen, the Boise, Idaho, company with very wide-ranging railroad business interests, including civil engineering and consultancy worldwide, also took up contract rebuilding. Morrison-Knudsen tried in 1978 to escape dependence on EMD or GE spares by adopting for four Southern Pacific General Electric U25B remanufactures the Sulzer engine widely used in Europe. Its hope was to popularize the Sulzer range in the US, but to date the move seems to have met with an unenthusiastic response.

Another factor in the size of the moth-balled locomotive fleet in the early 1980s was the drive for higher operating efficiency throughout the railroad industry. That had two stimuli. First was the staggering rise in

Above: A GE 3,100hp C30-7A in Conrail colors.

diesel fuel cost, from 10 cents a gallon in the early 1970s to 35-40 cents by 1978, but then to a daunting $1 a gallon in 1981. Union Pacific calculated that between 1970 and 1980 the proportion of each revenue dollar from its railroad freight that was collared by fuel bills had jumped from 3 to 14 cents. Second was the need anyway to lower ton-mile running costs, especially to grasp the opportunities opened up by deregulation. The obvious course was to lay off older, fuel-hungry and costly-to-maintain machines, and to work with the minimum number of recent models. In the early 1980s Class I railroads were extracting at least 50 percent more transportation per dollar of maintenance expenditure from their locomotives than they had been in 1970.

By 1983, however, with global oil production again outrunning consumption, the price of a gallon of diesel fuel had eased back close to 80 cents a gallon. And Class I railroads generally were logging increased tonnage as the national economy revived. Would that end the desperately lean years of the builders: or would the railroads simply reactivate their stored locomotives?

First with a heartening answer was Conrail. Although 22 percent of its 3,240 locomotives were stored, it asto-

nished the industry by ordering from GM-EMD 40 3,500hp SD50 and from GE 60 3,700hp B36-7 units, total value $114 million, for delivery in late 1983; and then, toward the end of that year, putting in fresh orders for 40 more SD50s and, from GE, 50 C30-7A units and 10 of a new C32-8 design. How could it possibly justify such massive expenditure when so much idle horsepower was parked about its property?

The answer was partly generous long-term financing of the purchases by the builders, but the rest could not have pleased the builders more if they had articulated it themselves. No economically feasible remanufacture, argued Conrail, could secure all the technical advances in improved tractive effort and fuel efficiency offered in the latest models, or their lower maintenance costs. In fuel consumption alone the new machines would have a 10 percent advantage over Conrail's existing fleet. All in all, their reduced running costs would show a better return on the capital outlay incurred in their purchase than the outturn from rehabilitating pensioned-off units.

Before examining the new technology in detail, a brief survey of recent diesel traction history is desirable. From what has already been said, it is probably clear that the US locomotive market in every power category from 1,000hp yard switcher to high-horsepower line-haul unit, or road-switcher, is now monopolized by GM-EMD and GE; and, of late, GE, the younger by many years of the two so far as production of a full catalog of locomotive types is concerned, has come much closer to sharing the business with GM-EMD.

In Canada Bombardier and its Alco-based models built by the Montreal Locomotive Works contend with GM Canada. Bombardier hankers after US business and in March 1986 received an order from the New Jersey Transit Corporation for 20 commuter train cars. It was also commissioned to overhaul 147 cars of the same type. In November 1986 Southeastern Pennsylvania ordered 35 push-pull coaches and seven

diesel locos. In palmier days, when the North American orders were easier to come by, it had some technical cooperation from GE, but the GE of the 1980s is too preoccupied with maximizing the return on investment in its own Erie plant.

In the late 1960s, when tonnage was booming on many railroads, there was the makings of a horsepower race in the heavy-duty locomotive market. Its culmination was construction for Union Pacific by both GM-EMD and GE of what were basically units packaging on one frame the power plants and ancillaries of two road switchers. The theory underlying the concept, which originated with UP's Chief Mechanical Officer, was that any locomotive's independent mobility specifically influenced certain of its running costs. Therefore double-unit packaging ought to lower these substantially in relation to power output – more than enough, in fact, to offset the assuredly increased capital cost of a special-order mammoth compared to that of two off-the-shelf units offering the same total power rating.

So from 1963 to the end of the decade GE manufactured for UP two 5,000hp types that wrapped together two of the builder's U25 power assemblies; one was the U50 B+B-B+B (Southern Pacific also took three of these), and the other the U50C C-C, the heaviest machine of that layout ever produced in the US. GM-EMD's variations on the UP theme were first the 5,000hp DD35 cab and booster units of 1963-65, then the mighty 6,600hp DD40AX; both models were mounted on two four-axle bogies, and therefore D-D. Otherwise known as the "Centennial" type because its emergence coincided with UP's 1969 Centenary, the DD40AX is the only one of these four 5,000hp-plus designs to have survived into the 1980s, because the hoped-for economies in operation were never sufficiently realized to justify persistence with non-standard machines. Even the "Centennials" were stored as tonnage levels receded in the early 1980s – UP alone had 700 locomotives cocooned in 1982,

and even in mid-1984 as many as 328 – but 25 of the 32 still on UP's roster were reactivated when traffic revived early in 1984.

So in the 1970s the Class I railroads mostly settled for 3,000hp C-Cs for their heavy tonnage work. Many had been scared by operational unreliabilities and escalating maintenance costs through purchase of new models aiming to hoist power/weight ratios. Dependability and ease of upkeep were therefore top priorities.

Thus GM-EMD sold vastly more of its 3,000hp SD40-2 C-C with a 16-cylinder 645 series engine, both in the US and Canada, than of its 3,600hp SD45-2 with a 20-cylinder engine. The SD45-2 made a considerable sales impact when it was added to the GM-EMD catalog but found no takers after three years of production because of complaints that the extra 600hp was not worth the high maintenance costs experienced with the bigger engine. GE seemed to have stolen a march on its La Grange rival at the outset of the 1970s by pushing its 16-cylinder engine rating up to 3,600hp; but GE likewise found its 3,000hp U30 and subsequent C30-7 C-C far more saleable than the high-powered U36, which did not take long to stir up the same discontent as GM-EMD's 3,600hp C-C.

The "SD" in GM-EMD's type categorization stands for "Special Duty," "GP" for "General Purpose." Ironically, GP was becoming the more apt prefix for the 3,000hp C-C as the 1970s unfolded. The railroads' overriding concern for reliability had killed off interest in the desperate pursuit of high-horsepower four-axle units that for various reasons

Top left: Bombardier's 3,200hp Type HR616 for Canadian National with new air ducting system, for improved protection against winter snow getting into the machinery.

Top: A quartet of UP SD40-2s swings a freight over Clio trestle near Graeagle, California.

Above: UP is one of the railroads employing both GM-EMD and GE power. This unit coal train east of North Platte, Nebraska, has three GE 3,000hp C30-7s.

Left: Most powerful unit in GE's "Dash-7" range at the start of the 1980s; the 3,600hp C36-7, as supplied to Norfolk & Western.

had enthused them in the 1960s. The maintenance cost question apart, any operator working tonnage over sharply graded routes was putting a much higher premium on the sure-footedness of six motored axles than on the theoretical advantages of high power/locomotive weight ratios. The striking characteristic of the later 1970s in the traction market was the sharply rising proportion of C-Cs in total orders placed with the North American builders. By 1979 it was as high as 60 percent, as the C-C became the all-purpose unit of so many systems and major purchases of 2,300-3,000 B-Bs were generated only by railroads with easily-graded main lines. Many others were content to renew their B-B stocks by remanufacture.

With the 1980s and sky-high fuel prices, recession, and declining tonnage, satisfaction with six-axled units of 3,000hp became more qualified. The capital cost of new locomotives had risen sharply since the 1970s and with it, understandably, the gap between the price of four- and six-axle units had widened. Concern on this score was aggravated by the high interest rates of the period, which made financing of new purchases more expensive. Next, the exorbitant cost of diesel oil naturally highlighted the fact that a six-axle

unit added anything up to 50 tons per locomotive to the gross weight of a train, compared to use of B-Bs with equivalent power rating. If there were still grounds for misgivings about majoring on high-horsepower B-Bs or taking on sharply uprated C-C power plants, then the builders had to be badgered for contrivances that would enhance the usable tractive effort and fuel efficiency of more conservative types.

The manufacturers were, in fact, coming up with valuable aids in this respect. Their research and develop-

Left: GM-EMD 2,000hp SD20-2s straddle the hump of Chessie's big Queensgate Yard at Cincinnati, Ohio.

ment had secured some important advances since the end of the 1960s.

At La Grange the first step was GM-EMD's supercession of its pioneering 567 engine series with the improved 645. Then in early 1972 came rationalization of its line-haul locomotive catalog with concentration on five "Dash-2" models, so-called because the updated types concerned were designated with that suffix. They were the 2,000hp GP38-2 B-B and SD-38 C-C; 3,000hp GP40-2 and SD40-2 C-C; and the 3,600hp SD45-2 C-C. All had standardized ac/dc transmission – that, is alternator/rectifier generation of current for dc traction motors, a far more satisfactory means of accommodating high power than the previous system using a fast-running dc motor-generator as the link between diesel engine and dc traction motors; but ac/dc transmissions did not become feasible until solid state electronics compacted the size of alternator/rectifier assemblies sufficiently for use in a locomotive without intolerable weight and bulk penalties.

Electronics also figured in the most heavily-promoted "Dash-2" improvement, a completely redesigned electrical system that both increased its operating capacity and simplified maintenance, the latter by applying electronic modules to each of its elements. But in addition many engine, engine accessory, and transmission components were revised and the C-Cs were mounted on a new pattern of high-adhesion truck which, through interaction of a new type of motor and body suspension, reduced wheel-slip risks and thus bolstered tractive effort at starting and acceleration. That innovation was clearly a major step down the road to improved fuel efficiency; it allowed more tonnage to be hung on a "Dash-2's" coupler than its unsuffixed antecedent could reliably manage.

GE's developing model range displayed many improvements with similar objectives during the 1970s. In 1977 this company adopted a type designation code which makes the dating and power/wheel arrangement identification of a GE type child's play. Description of each type starts with a letter indicating wheel arrangement; then come two digits denoting horsepower rating (rounded up), and finally, after a dash, a single digit representing decade of introduction. Thus after updating GE's 2,205hp U23B B-B was transmuted into the B23-7 in 1977, its 3,000hp U30B B-B into the B30-7 and its 3,000hp U30C C-C into the C30-7, to cite three examples. Incidentally, one cardinal point of difference in GE and GM-EMD practice ought to be noted: GE uses four-stroke engines, whereas GM-EMD has resolutely stuck with the two-stroke principle.

By the dawn of the 1980s both major US builders – and Bombardier in Canada – had developed adhesion aids to a degree that persuaded numerous railroads to invest in high-horsepower B-Bs and in higher-rated C-Cs. All had the same objective, technically known as creep control. An accelerating locomotive develops anything up to 25 percent less tractive force if there is no trace of slippage between powered wheel and rail than it does if the wheel is "creeping" into a slight, steady slip. But that "creep" must be strictly controlled at a rate that differs no more than 1-2mph from the pace of wheel rotating without any slippage at all.

GM-EMD's Adhesion Control System obtains this creep control by electronic comparison of readings from a radar unit mounted beneath the locomotive, which reports true ground speed by continuously scanning the roadbed, with those of another device calculating traction motor speed. The relationship of the two sets of data is processed automatically to generate command for power reduction precisely measured to

hold creep at the ideal level for maximum effort; if the variation is considerable, application of sand to the rail may be automatically prescribed as well. GE's Sentry Adhesion System is based on sensitive detection of any wheel-slip and the latter's prompt control by automatic sanding; this does not permit as much creep as the GM-EMD apparatus claims to allow.

The GM-EMD device was one of the features of its "Super Series" models embodying a new turbocharged refinement of the 645 engine, the 645F3, which were premiered in 1981 and have attracted several large-scale buyers. The "Super Series" are the GP50 B-B and SD50 C-C, both 3,500hp units; in each case the high output is extracted from a 16-cylinder engine. GE's system is a vital auxiliary of the B36-7 and C36-7 which it put on the market in the early 1980s to rival the "Super Series," and with marked success; the C36-7 was being sold rated as highly as 3,750hp.

Both the US manufacturing giants unveiled new locomotive model ranges in 1984, GE its "Dash-8" series and GM-EMD its "60" series. The technological development of each new line had similar emphases.

GM-EMD's offerings all embody its new 710G series of engines, a further

stage in the evolution of its characteristic turbocharged, two-stroke cycle power plant. During its 1980-83 period of production GM-EMD hoisted the fuel efficiency of the previous model by 7 percent in its final 645F version. The 16-cylinder 710G is claimed to step up the improvement a further 5 percent. Apart from advances in component design, such as its new pattern of turbocharger, it is ingenious measures to limit what are called "parasitic power losses" – that is, engine output bled off to motor equipment like radiator fans and traction motor blowers – that notably contribute to rising fuel efficiency.

Bigger cylinder displacement and the new turbocharger are the key factors in the 710G's traction rating of 3,800hp (GM-EMD says it has scope for still higher rating) and a new type of traction motor has been produced to absorb this output. That is the figure at which the 710G is applied to the 390,000lb six-axle SD60, a unit for heavy-duty or medium-speed main-line freight hauls, and the 260,000lb four-axle GP60, conceived for intermediate- or high-speed freight service. An SD59 and GP59 are

Below: The ultimate in four-axle power; GE's 3,900hp B39-8, one of its new "Dash-8" range of the mid-1980s.

also on the market with lower-rated 710G engines.

GE's new model line comprises a 2,300hp B23-8, a 3,170hp B32-8, a 3,910hp B39-8, a 3,150hp C32-8, and a 3,890hp C39-8. The two 39-8 types have the 16-cylinder version, the remainder the 12-cylinder variant of the company's FDL engine coupled to a new design of alternator and powering upgraded models of the long-running GE 752 traction motor. Comparable gains of efficiency under various heads as for GM-EMD's new range are proclaimed for the "Dash-8s." The B39-8, for which Santa Fe was the first customer, is the most powerful four-motor diesel in US history.

Common to both manufacturers' new product ranges is more sophisticated application of microcomputer electronics to control systems. The product is yet more simplification of a locomotive's electrics, more precise control of all functions, and invaluable aids to maintenance that reduce locomotive downtime in shops, not only through fresh advances in modular electronic circuitry but also through diagnostic applications of new technology.

Taking the GM-EMD arrangement

Below: Computerized loco simulator at the Chessie engineer-training school.

as an example, this employs two separate microcomputers to interface with the main control systems and ensure their operation at maximum efficiency. One, known as the logic system, deals with the engine, power generation, and traction motors and their response to the engineer's movements of his cab controls. The other, called the excitation system, gets information from the logic system in commands it has passed and feedback on equipment response, on the basis of which it controls such items as the creep control, dynamic brake, and new fuel economy devices.

A third microcomputer performs a "diagnostic and display" function. This is continuously monitoring the locomotive's performance, detecting abnormal conditions, recording the conditions of

Above: Light duty switcher: GE Type SL144 with two Cummins 550hp engines.

the locomotive at the time any fault occurs or looks incipient, and in some cases automatically initiates corrective action. It has an archive module that intercommunicates with the other two microcomputers to maintain a permanent record of vital operational data, such as mileage, duty cycle, and traction motor loadings. All this clearly provides shop staff with instant advice on where to probe for a fault and how it should be tackled when a defective locomotive trundles in. For the engineer on the road, too, the "display" part of the systems function is far more informative than his traditional cab cluster of fault annunciators and lights. He now has a four-line panel of indicators to keep him briefed both on the status of more of the locomotive's equipment and also on the nature and location of faults to which previous cab displays had no access.

There is no space to discuss in detail the range of modestly-powered, 1,000-1,500hp switchers employed in many a yard and terminal, and on countless smaller US railroads, but two kinds of unmanned locomotive demand cursory attention.

One is the popularly tagged "slug" or, in GE's more euphonious acronym, MATE – "Motors to Assist Tractive Effort," which fully explains the "slug's" purpose. Adhesion constraints, as earlier discussion has implied, pre-

vent even a six-axle, six-motor locomotive making full use of the electric power generated by the power plant when a trainload is started from rest. More of that power can be utilized, naturally, if it is distributed to a greater number of motored axles. Hence the "slug" concept, which is essentially a unit with motored trucks and a superstructure to house their necessary auxiliaries, such as traction motor cooling blowers, but no prime diesel engine/alternator mover; power is generated by a parent locomotive.

"Slugs" add non-revenue-earning weight to an operation, so they are not a sensible solution to any requirement for tougher tractive effort. Their use is limited to boosting the effort of yard switchers, which are frequently called upon to maneuver at slow speed tonnages which would overtax their own rating; and to line-haul situations where speed is limited but extra adhesion is invaluable.

"Slugs" must not be confused with booster units. The latter are fully engined traction units, but cabless for economy's sake because their railroad owners regard their likely use in everything but multiple-unit formations as highly improbable. Burlington Northern, for example, deploys 120 cabless versions of GE's B30-7 (the boosters are designated B30-7A). Another recent BN practice worth mention is its conversion of surplus tank cars to serve as

25-gallon auxiliary tankers for diesel locomotives. Coupling one of these tankers to a four-locomotive formation on a Chicago-Seattle run, BN has found, eliminates five fueling stops en route. Another virtue of the tanker is that it enables heavy-axleload locomotives to service lightweight-rail branches from which such machines would normally be debarred, because 80 percent of the locomotive's usual fuel tankload can be carried in the tanker, thereby trimming more than 11 tons from the locomotive's usual weight in full working order.

Southern, Southern Pacific, Kansas Southern, Seaboard, and Union Pacific are US railroads which, along with some Canadian systems mentioned in the chapter on that country, use "slave" locomotives. "Slaves" are helper locomotives that are unmanned and remotely-controlled by radio from the lead unit fronting a train. Their insertion in mid-train facilitates operation of longer trains – particularly valuable when otherwise the volume of traffic might saturate a single line's capacity by distributing drawbar forces, achieving better control of coupling slack through the train, and improving braking response, because the through-train air pipe is being charged from two widely separated sources and pressure is created more quickly toward the rear of the train; in reverse, the release of brakes is likewise better coordinated.

Above left: AM-EMD 1,100hp SW1001 switcher for SP at Long Beach dockside, California.
Above: Sante Fe switcher and "slug" combine to work Barstow Yard.
Above right: One of BN's cabless GE B30-7A boosters.
Right: Three of Alaska Railroad's GM-EMD F-7 units swing its tourist special 297ft above the water on Hurricane Gulch bridge.

Locotrol is the radio control system now employed in all "slave" systems. It has just the same capacity for transmission of commands as the 27-point jumper cable with which locomotives are linked for single, head-end control in a multiple-unit formation. In the controlling, or master, locomotive's cab the engineer has an additional console covering the "slave(s)" with a selector switch through which he can set up either instantaneous, matching response of the "slave(s)" to any movement by him of the master locomotive's controls – in other words, have the "slave(s)" working multiple-unit as though they were jumper cable-coupled to the "master" – or else separate control of the "slave(s)." Separate control is useful for train management in some ticklish track situations, where it may pay to have head-end units under power and "slave(s)" in the dynamic braking mode – that is, with their motors reversed, thereby opposing momentum by turning into generators

of current which is absorbed by banks of resistance. Visual displays in the master unit's cab confirm the state of all vital controls in the "slave(s)" and report any key faults; these displays are actuated also by radio signals, automatically generated on the "slave(s)."

So far this chapter has been occupied exclusively with freight power. The mainstay of national passenger operator Amtrak's diesel fleet is GM-EMD's 3,000hp F40PH B-B, a full-width body, or "cowl", unit. Amtrak originally bought a large fleet of C-Cs, the SDP40F, that were essentially fast freight units slightly modified for passenger duty. But these intended replacements for Amtrak's inherited, elderly GM-EMD E and F series streamlined units soon showed in a series of derailments that their three-axle trucks and carbody weight distribution were not suited to passenger train pace over the indifferently maintained tracks of many Amtrak routes in the early 1970s, especially through curves. Eventually Amtrak was driven to scrap or trade most of a once 150-strong SDP40F fleet against an expanded construction of the more track compatible FP40H, which Amtrak had originally bought to serve only its short-haul services. Starting with Chicago's Regional Transit Authority (RTA), some of the agencies throughout the country which furnish the equipment for railroad commuter operation under contract have also invested in the FP40H.

Treasured by all rail buffs, a few of the streamline-nosed full-width body GM-EMD F series of locomotives from the late 1940s and early 1950s were still active in late 1983. US Class I railroads with Fs still on their books included the Alaska, Soo, Southern, and Seaboard, while both CN and CP Rail in Canada retained examples. Other US operators were one or two of the regional US transportation authorities such as: Massachusetts (MBTA), deploying former Gulf Mobile & Ohio F3As and F7As rebuilt into FP10s at

Illinois Central Gulf's Paducah shops; Maryland (MDOT) with ex-Baltimore & Ohio F7As reconditioned as F9Hs by Morrison-Knudsen; and New Jersey with F7s leased from Chicago & North Western.

The aggravation of soaring oil costs by oil shortages at the end of the 1970s naturally aroused the proponents of rail electrification. Some of the arguments put for its energy-efficiency were more dramatic than scientific, and took precious little account of electrification's greater economic relevance to the densely-trafficked double-track main lines of Europe than to a North American single track passing massive freight trains at far less frequent intervals. Nevertheless, in its twilight the Carter Administration was prompted to float a scheme for Federal financing of US trunk route electrification, with the underwriting of the fixed installations to be repaid by per-ton royalties on the traffic which the ultimately electrified lines carried. Even if the oil crisis worsened – which, of course, it did not – such a scheme was certain to be marked off for the trash-can by the incoming Reagan Administration. It is now just a footnote to railroad history.

So the only North American mainline electrification in the mid-1980s remains the ex-Pennsylvania and New Haven catenary in the Northeast Corridor, which is discussed in the next chapter on Amtrak. In addition to metros, there is some electric operation of US surface commuter services in territory administered by the regional authorities. Among the most notable of those authorities are New Jersey, New

Above: GM-EMD's passenger power: an FP40H in GO Transit service, on the Richmond Hill line near downtown Toronto, heading a rake of the Ontario authority's distinctive bi-levels.
Right: Enter electric traction: one of BC Rail's new 50kV locomotives, No. 5007, is hauled over CP rail to the newly electrified Tumbler Ridge branch in British Columbia.

York, and Southeastern Pennsylvania. Burlington Northern, Canadian Pacific, and Missouri-Kansas-Texas are the three railroads which principally reiterate that they keep the case for electrification perennially under methodical review, but none of them see the arguments in favor firming significantly. Until Canada's British Columbia recently electrified its new Tumbler Ridge branch, as described in Chapter 8, the only postwar North American electrification scheme of potentially trendsetting significance was undertaken in Arizona, as part of the Navajo Power Project. There a 78-mile line, the Black Mesa & Lake Powell Railroad, was laid from the Kayenta coalfield to an electricity generating station to serve as a conveyor belt-like coal feed and electrified at 50kV 60Hz. The line is worked by a pair of hopper-car train-sets, each completing three or four round trips daily, and hauled by GE-built 6,600hp C-C electrics.

A comeback for steam sounds a far-fetched possibility, but it is not quite unimaginable. At today's oil-price levels a reliable coal-burning steam locomotive attaining only half the thermal efficiency of a diesel could cut deep into a Class I railroad's operating bill, even though it costs more than a diesel to keep in good trim. An Argentinian

locomotive engineer, Dante Porta, has come up with new thoughts in steam locomotive technology which, applied to a South African Railways 4-8-2, have indicated through practical use of the modified locomotive on a South African main line the possibility that a new generation of such steam machines could trim present costs of operating traffic with diesel traction by a thumping 70 percent.

Back in 1980 a concern named American Coal Enterprises promoted a design, ACE-3000, embodying the principal feature of Porta's theory, a fire-grate in which the coal is gasified, somewhat as in a coke oven, to minimize combustion losses. Its boiler would generate 300lb/sq in steam for four cylinders employing a Walschaerts valve gear with microprocessor-controlled cut-off control, and working on compound expansion principles. Other innovations too numerous to list in full would include exhaust gas expulsion through the stack by a steam turbine, and feedwater heating by condensation of exhausted steam. Wheel layout of the locomotive would be 4-4-4-2, with each pair of driving axles linked to one pair of cylinders, and for compatibility with diesels the machine would be double-ended, with a cab-in-front locomotive and cab-in-rear tender (which in the version of the concept designated 3000-8 would also be powered).

At one time Burlington Northern and Chessie were patrons of this enterprise, but by 1984 both had dropped out because of disagreement over finance of a prototype's detailed design and construction, which was likely to absorb at least £50 million. That left ACE-3000 firmly on the drawing board, still in need of a godfather. But BN's interest in coal-burning remained lively. In alliance with fellow coal haulier Norfolk Southern it was supporting GE's research in this area. This ranged from systems mixing diesel and micropulverized coal to fluidized-bed combustion together with new coal or gas turbine possibilities.

7
AMTRAK PULLS THROUGH

Just about the only glimmer of hope for the US intercity passenger train's long-term survival in the second half of the 1960s was the effort to sustain a high-speed New York-Washington service in the populous Northeast Corridor, under the shelter of the Johnson Administration's High Speed Ground Transportation Act of 1965. True, by 1969 Congress had been roused to the imminence of a final curtain on the tragedy wherein some 15,000 daily services of the late 1930s had been steadily ground down to little more than 500. But it was confronted, under Nixon, with an Office of Management & Budget that flatly opposed any significant Federal life-support apparatus.

Eventually the Administration was outvoted and legislation of October 1970 created a Federally-subsidized corporation, subsequently known as Amtrak, to manage a slender, rationalized long-haul network of service delineated by Washington. Initially this operation, launched at the end of April 1971, embraced 21 routes running no more than 184 daily trains. Railroads still operating passenger trains had the option of transacting an Amtrak takeover, including transfer of their passenger cars and locomotives, or carrying on at their own cost with no chance of opting out for several years. The only standouts were Rock Island, Southern, and Denver & Rio Grande Western, but all three later made over their residual workings to Amtrak. The last to bow to the high cost of running its own train as a prestige symbol was D&RGW, which terminated its much admired Denver-Salt Lake City "Rio Grande Zephyr" in 1983. Amtrak owned no main-line track of its own outside the Northeast Corridor. For the efficient operation of its trains elsewhere it

was wholly dependent on the goodwill of host railroads, their operations staff and their men assigned to crew Amtrak's trains.

Amtrak was not sent into the world with any legislative conviction that it would ever be self-supporting financially. On the other hand, it was never expected to be as hungry for Federal dollars as it was in its first decade, when one way or another it soaked up almost $6½ billion and each Amtrak traveler was reckoned to have his fare subsidized by as much as $40 on average.

Inflation and soaring oil prices were unforeseeable factors in Amtrak's need of a steadily rising operational subsidy, as were two phenomenally hard winters, 1976-77 and 1978-79, which ravaged performance. But the upward climb of maintenance costs was no surprise. While Amtrak was granted enough capital to begin renewal of its shorter-haul cars with a non-powered version of the Budd-built "Metroliner" electric mu car devised for the Northeast Corridor project (the Amcoach and its kin subsequently configured within the same bodyshell, the Amcafes, Amlounges, and so on), on longer-haul routes it was forced to make do and mend with steam-heated streamliner cars that were already worn out and malfunction-prone when they were entrusted to Amtrak.

Not that trouble-free and proven equipment could be bought off the shelf when Amtrak had money in its hand. With the passenger train seemingly on hellbent skids, US industry had naturally dropped any purposeful research

Right: Three FP40Hs hustle the eastbound "California Zephyr" of Amtrak through Fruita, western Colorado. Bi-level "Superliners" dominate the consist.

Left: Four refurbished Metroliner railcars hurry through Lanham, Maryland, in the years when they were covering the New York-Washington service.

and design work in that traction and vehicle area. Nor was there anyone on the operating side of railroading with updated experience in drafting specifications for passenger equipment.

The equipment was all too painfully experienced in the "Metroliner" electric mus ordered by committee, which had been ordered (a sure recipe for catastrophe in any circumstances) before Amtrak's birth. Vehicle and electrical equipment builders had been handed an absurdly ambitious requirement that, among other things, demanded ability to accelerate from rest to 150mph within three minutes on level track, whereas at that juncture much of the Northeast Corridor route was rarely fit for 100mph, and to hold the same pace up a 1 percent grade. The outcome was cars with every axle motored for a stupendous short-burst output of 640hp per vehicle, but ones packed with so much innovation unproven in regular rail service that they were immediately plagued with trou-

ble. It took a year to make any of them acceptable for scheduled public service, in 1969; and two years more before enough of the 61-strong fleet was deemed competent enough to begin a seven-train-each-way daily service between New York and Washington. Eventually, later in the 1970s, all 61 cars were perforce submitted to a modification program of almost 100 items at a cost of more than $500,000 apiece, which made them fully but expensively reliable (and after which, in July 1974, one was demonstrated to perform smoothly at up to 152mph).

For lack of a continuing thread of US design for passenger work, Amtrak's own first traction purchases were just as ill-starred, with the exception of its Turboliners. In the early 1970s, when fuel was cheap, some European railways were convinced that the aerospace industry's lightweight turbine engines, developed principally for helicopters, were the coming propulsion for high-speed trains, because of this pow-

er plant's high output in relation to size and weight. French Railways took on a fleet of turbine-electric train-sets; and of the second French design, known as the Type RTG, Amtrak imported six units then had seven more built under license, with a few detail differences, by Rohr in California. These were Rohr's last essays in rail car building.

The Turboliners still perform satisfactorily, and at 100-110mph where track allows, as it has done west of Albany after the Rohr-built sets' New York-Buffalo via Albany itinerary had by 1980 been partly relaid and resignaled with New York state funding raised through an electorally-supported bond issue. But oil price escalation has completely destroyed the turbine's economy in railtraction, even after substitution of a Rohr Turboliner's original two 1,100hp engines by a single 1,600hp unit. The book has been closed on European development and France's only export sales since the Amtrak buy have been four trains to Iran in 1975-76 and three to Egypt in 1982-83. Because of their suddenly hoisted fuel costs, the four French sets were taken out of their Midwest service in 1982, but they too were rebuilt with a single engine and returned to operations in 1987.

Locomotive buying was Amtrak's minefield. Seeking a replacement for the Northeast Corridor's venerated but venerable ex-Pennsylvania GGI electric locomotives, Amtrak could only take from General Electric what was essentially the reworking of a recent freight locomotive design for the newly ac-electrified Black Mesa & Lake Powell industrial railroad in Arizona. Because of their chronic disagreement with track at high speed, three 32 6,000hp E60s were eventually limited

Left: Amtrak Turboliner.

Right: An Amtrak 6,000hp E60 electric Co-Co.

by the Federal Railroad Administration to 90mph in the Northeast Corridor, which hopelessly circumscribed their relevance to that route's projected high-speed development. By 1984 a number had been sold off, mostly to New Jersey Transit Rail's commuter operation.

At the end of the 1970s Amtrak sensibly bought foreign electric traction technology that had been methodically developed and proven in passenger duty. The machine was the AEM-7 5,000hp Bo-Bo of only 100.8 tons' weight, otherwise known as the "Mickey Mouse" or "Little Volvo" because these GM-built locomotives are a derivation of Swedish electrical conglomerate ASEA's long line of Type Rc locomotives for Swedish State Railways. The 47 AEM-7s and their Amfleet consists now dominate the New York-Washington high-speed service, having exiled the "Metroliner" mus to the New York/Philadelphia-Harrisburg route.

The same traumas of derailments attributable to a basically freight design's discomfort with high-speed on characteristic US track harassed the 3,000hp SPD40F Co-Co that Amtrak obtained from GM-EMD to supersede the aging E and F diesels it had inherited. In 1976, these mishaps provoked the Federal Railroad Administration to clap a 40mph limit almost nationwide on the SPD40Fs' negotiation of two-degree or sharper curves. That forced Amtrak to bite the bullet and trade in the six-axle machines for very costly manufacture as the four-axle F40PH type which it had subsequently had GM-EMD custom-design for passenger duty, though originally Amtrak had conceived the F40PH purely as shorter-haul traction.

Right: The "Little Volvo": an Amtrak AEM-7 electric Bo-Bo.

These troubles were handy ammunition for critics already firing freely enough at Amtrak. The snipers were not only the competing bus operators but more than one railroad, resentful at having to preserve track space for passenger trains when the energy crisis was promising a bonanza of coal tonnage in particular. There was still more resentment at heavy Federal funding for a concern clinging to a meager 1-2 percent of the national intercity passenger market while railroads were scratching just a percent return or less from the private capital they had invested in a freight operation of vastly more national economic significance. In some cases their irritation was expressed in cavalier operating treatment of Amtrak trains: that blatantly flouted a clause in Amtrak's founding legislation

which banned railroads from favoring freight over passenger trains except in an emergency.

The crunch came in 1979, when an economy-bent Carter Administration sought to hack away over 40 percent of the expanded route network which Amtrak had by then been permitted to develop; to cut Amtrak's services as expressed in annual train-miles by a third; and to hike Amtrak fares so that none were more than 50 percent subsidized. But the timing was wrong.

That summer the Iranian revolution sparked an oil supply crisis. Frustrated and furious car-owners were confronted by empty gas stations, and for Amtrak ticket sales it was temporarily bingo. Astute lobbying by Amtrak galvanized key Senators and Representatives into unyielding defense of

threatened services in their respective electoral backyards. In fact, both House and Senate all but voted to freeze the existing route structure intact, but at the end of the day a 17 percent route-map trimming was approved. Out went the Chicago-Miami "Floridian," the Chicago-Houston "Lone Star," the New York-Kansas City "National Limited," and the Chicago-Seattle "North Coast Hiawatha," plus the notoriously politic-al Washington-Roanoke-Catlettsburg "Hilltopper," a commercially absurd operation that owed its being almost entirely to the influence of a powerful Washington legislator. But several important routes, by the Carter plan, such as Washington-New Orleans and Chicago-Los Angeles via the Santa Fe, were reprieved.

Congress did more. Besides upping the levels of both operating subsidy and capital investment support for Amtrak, it raised substantially the Federal start-up money on offer for "403(b)" services. That tag refers to a clause in the founding Amtrak legislation which encouraged states to put up their own dollars for whatever might be needed by way of track improvements or equip-ment, then to subsidize operating costs for local Amtrak services they hank-ered after, but which were not held to justify the full level of Federal aid. To get a 403(b) service off the ground, Federal dollars were now to be had for as much as 80 percent of the first year's costs, 65 percent for the second year's and 50 percent per annum thereafter. Among other things, this new generos-ity turned some railroad hearts a little warmer toward Amtrak, since it hinted at the possibility of more public money being plowed into track and signaling betterments from which a railroad's

freight trains were bound to extract some free benefit.

Of the many 403(b) exercises in numerous states, the most conspicuously successful is California's between Los Angeles and San Diego. Launched in the 128-mile corridor in 1976 on a thrice-daily basis, the service has justified expansion to seven trains each way (though Santa Fe had to be hard-pressed by the state to accommodate the seventh addition to traffic over its tracks).

By the start of the 1980s Amtrak had its act pretty well together. Its annual tally of passengers had passed the 20 million mark. More importantly from the political viewpoint, the take from each traveler was rising. In 1978 Amtrak was meeting only 38.5 percent of its full costs out of revenue, but by 1982 it had raised the proportion to 50 percent – three years ahead of the target year for that achievement set by Congress, incidentally – and by early 1984 the mark was as high as 56 percent. The direct running costs of the trains were being covered as much as 80 percent as mid-decade approached.

Also under way was re-equipment of

Far left, above: Superliner family bedroom, windowed both sides, extends the full width of the car.

Center: Superliner diner has the restaurant on the upper level, the kitchen below.

Above: Superliner de luxe bedroom.

Below: Amtrak "403(b)" service: California state-supported Oakland-Bakersfield "San Joaquin" at Martinez.

long-haul trains like the "Pioneer," "Southwest Limited," "Coast Starlight," "Sunset Limited" and "San Francisco Zephyr" with elegant new "Superliner" bilevels, 284 of them, built by Pullman-Standard. Yet again Amtrak did not escape trouble with the new equipment, as Superliner delivery was badly delayed by labor disputes at the builders and then by some teething snags with the cars' equipment. Once they were in service, the stately Superliners, riding on German-pattern air-suspension trucks, won Amtrak new market respect. Their sleeper accommodation ranged from neat economy bedrooms through full-width family bedrooms with space for up to three adults and two children, to de luxe bedrooms with private toilets; some bedrooms could open up into a pleasing suite by removing a partition. The Superliner diner had an 18-table, 72-seat saloon above, an all-electric kitchen below; and the Sightseer lounge a 46-seater glazed-roof bar-lounge on the upper deck, a 26-seater cafe-lounge on the ground floor.

Several routes in the eastern US had clearances too tight for the Superliners, as they had been for the dome cars of the old streamliners. As it could not afford simultaneously to re-equip those trains with less generously-contoured diners and sleepers, Amtrak had to update their existing cars on one count if no other. The Superliners were built with all-electric equipment, including heating, to be fed by train line from the locomotive: and the FP40H diesels had been built with the means solely to supply electrical train auxiliaries. So steam car heating had to go.

That was the genesis of what Amtrak now brands as its "Heritage Fleet." Starting in the late 1970s, Amtrak had by the end of 1984 revamped almost 600 of the cars it inherited in 1971 with all-electric equipment to be powered from the train's head-end. Over 100 more cars were slated for the same treatment. Although Amtrak

Above: Amtrak Los Angeles-Las Vegas-Ogden "Desert Wind" features, after the lead baggage car, "Heritage Fleet" sleeper, Amdinette and Superliner bi-levels.

had thus modernized some of the double-deck "Hi-Level" cars which once graced Santa Fe's "El Capitan," no one had given extended life for former streamliner dome cars much credence once Superliners were commissioned. Consequently surprised dome buffs purred when Amtrak unexpectedly committed seven Budd-built, former Northern Pacific domes to refurbishing and "Heritage Fleet" treatment in 1983, the first of them for the Chicago-Washington "Capitol Limited": more dome cars were similarly rejuvenated in 1985.

In 1980 Amtrak could summon up the resources to buy 150 more single-level cars for its eastern and southern routes. At that juncture it decided to stick with Budd and the basic Amfleet car design, though with some modifica-

Above: The upper level of an Alaska Railroad dome car.

tion for longer-haul work, so as to accelerate production. Three years later, however, Amtrak set about firming up wholly new designs that would eventually consign the entire "Heritage Fleet" to the scrapyards.

The new concept's interior is more capacious than an Amfleet car's, because the latter appropriated the metroliner mu body-shell pattern which had to sacrifice headroom to allow for a roof-mounted pantograph to collect traction current. In the new single-level sleeper particularly, day seating space below upper berths does not need to be so cramped. One novel feature of the new design is two tiers of windows, affording a view out of both upper and lower sleeping berths, but equally a sight-seeing advantage in day cars.

Amtrak was braced for a fresh political assault when the Reagan Administration won its first term, since in the election run-up Reagan's men had clearly targeted public transport for cuts in Federal expenditure. Soon after the poll, early in 1981, a transportation policy task force duly zeroed in on Amtrak. A scathing report issued from Office of Management & Budget Director David Stockman ranked the passenger train as expendable as a paddleboat: subsidized rail passenger service was damned as inappropriate because "the private sector offers common-carrier bus and air travel services" – an argument which blithely ignored the public money applied to the infrastructure and support systems of both alternative modes.

The Administration's first Budget consequently called for an immediate cut of a third in total Amtrak financing. A subsequent Bill sent to Congress presented a series of tapering cuts that would have slashed Amtrak support down to $350 million by 1986 (as against $993 million in the Carter Administration's last proposal for 1982, which was of course aborted). It also sought to burden states with the full cost of any capital works involved in 403(b) service start-ups, but not the total Federal withdrawal of support for all 403(b) operations except those crossing state lines which Reagan's men had originally threatened.

Arguing that "the costs of increasing train speed outweigh the benefits," the White House also moved to save $310 million on the chequered Northeast Corridor Improvement Program (NECIP), which must now be considered in more detail. Refurbishing of the electrified Pennsylvania-New York-Washington and part-electrified New Haven-Boston-New York routes had been activated under the Johnson era's 1965 High Speed Ground Transportation Act, in the hope of checking the clutter of the corridor's skies by airline shuttles and pollution of its surface by yet more cars, trucks, and buses.

This was the phase which produced

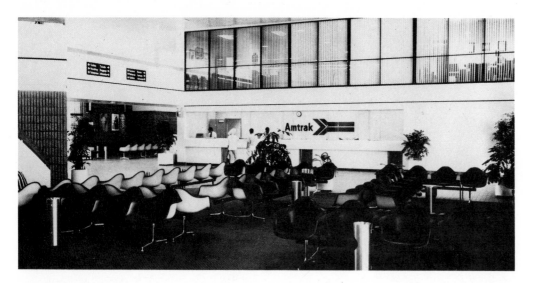

the Metroliner electric mus. By the start of the 1970s, with most of their infancy failings remedied, they were competently furnishing a seven-trains-each-way-daily New York-Washington service that featured some of the fastest contemporary schedules in the world league tables, notably a 43-minute timing for the 68.4 miles from Baltimore to Wilmington that demanded an average speed of 95.4mph start-to-stop. For the first time in almost 20 years Americans were riding trains making three-figure pace, up to as much as 115mph.

With Penn-Central's collapse and the need to restructure Northeast railroading, Congress took the view that since the Northeast Corridor's traffic was more intensive than its freight – a balance unique among North American trunk routes – this was a case where passenger operators should be the landlords and freight operators the tenants of trackage rights, not the converse which obtained elsewhere in Amtrak's network. The Ford Administration fought the idea tooth and nail, but Congress prevailed. Except for New York area mileage where the local transportation authorities became sovereign, the whole route from Boston to Washington, along with its stations and assorted maintenance facilities, was knocked down to Amtrak at a price that sent Penn-Central stockholders and creditors apopletic.

The Ford Administration did, however, determinedly resist pressures to fund a grandscale reconstruction of the Northeast Corridor main as a 150mph railroad. The 4-R Act of 1976 kept sights down to a maximum of 125mph.

Even so funding had to be hoisted to a total of £1.75 billion to cover a Northeast Corridor Improvement Program (NECIP) that provided for extension of electrification to Boston from the wires' existing finish at New Haven, on top of a thorough-going track reconstruction, realignment of particularly speed-constraining curves, bridge strengthening, and resignaling.

By the end of the 1970s the NECIP was on a cost runaway, largely because in earlier years its direction had been entrusted to an unwieldy mix of Feds, railroad men, and consulting engineers, a certain recipe for infighting, buck passing, and waste. So in 1979 the NECIP budget was raised to $2.5 billion. At the same time pruning began, notably with abandonment of the plan to convert the ex-Pennsylvania 12kV 25Hz electrification south of New York to the 25kV 60Hz which the New York Metropolitan Transportation Authority (MTA) was determined to substitute for the ex-New Haven 11kV 25Hz north of New York, and which was to be installed from New Haven on to Boston.

In its drive to cut the Federal outlay on Amtrak, the incoming Reagan administration succeeded in lopping that $310 million off the NECIP's $2.5 billion. Out went the New Haven-Boston electrification and most of the resignaling north of New York that was associated with it – wasting a great deal of planning work already done on both projects, incidentally – but although resignaling schemes south of New York were also driven into modification, the effect here was not significant in terms of future speed potential or operating efficiency. From Wilmington, Dela-

ware, on to Washington, where the often double-track route carries an intensive mix of passenger and freight trains that poses severe dispatching problems, the whole operation would still be placed under the control of a very sophisticated CTC devised by Chrysler Electronics (one of its novelties is the display to the center's dispatchers of the whole area's track layout by projection TV).

Completion of the entire NECIP was unlikely before the end of 1987 whereas, in the 1970s, 1981 had been the euphorically promised year of execution. But by the end of 1986 the track-work at least was 99 percent achieved, the bridge strengthening or reconstruction at least 93 percent done. As a result 275 miles of the route could be passed for 125 mph top speed during 1987 and the remainder was scheduled for clearance at the same pace within the near future. With that, some southbound "Metroliners" could have their Wilmington-Baltimore timing shaved down to 41 minutes, equivalent to a start-to-stop average speed of 101mph. Amtrak does not now aim to push Corridor speed any higher than 120mph, nor to lower New York-Washington journey time beyond 2½ hours.

Up to mid-decade Amtrak's story in the 1980s was one of assiduous lobbying and solidifying of Congressional relationships to keep the Reagan Administration's annual attempts to curtail its funding within manageable proportions. In this it was helped by the rising respect for its management, by the steadily improving reliability of its train services, and not least by its hold on a market of 19-20 million passenger journeys a year despite ever-fiercer competition over its longer routes from airlines sharply discounting fares.

Nevertheless, the total of Federal support for Amtrak was reduced some 25 percent in the early 1980s compared with the amounts budgeted in the twilight of the Carter Administration. Amtrak was compelled to make some draconian cuts in administrative staff. In a more ill-advised reaction Amtrak also cut out on-train diner dish preparation and resorted to microwave-oven resuscitation of pre-cooked entrees, served with disposable tableware. That sparked such a blaze of anger that Amtrak was soon forced to recant. By 1984 up to 80 percent of diner meals were once more being fashioned on train and decently presented.

At the start of 1984 Amtrak was deploying its trains over 44 main routes, still improving and adding to the stations they served, and also expanding its operation, chiefly with the encouragement of more state support under the 403(b) provisions. Thus, for instance, 1984 saw introduction of the "Pere Marquette" between Grand Rapids and Chicago, and of the North Carolina-backed "Piedmont" between Richmond, Raleigh, Greensboro, and Charlotte.

In 1983 Amtrak added the Auto Train to its portfolio of services. Since the mid-1950s Europe's railroads have expanded into a popular, Continent-wide network the concept of a train combining day, sleeper, and diner accommodation for car parties with rack cars for their autos, so as to eliminate the hassle of long drives, especially for families vacation-bound in summer, when highways are crowded and driving is penance. In the 1970s a private company launched a similar operation between Lorton, Virginia – a convenient railhead for a substantial eastern seaboard market – and Sanford, Florida. This prospered, but the company then aggravated an underlying problem of its undercapitalization by opening up a second route to Florida from Louisville, Kentucky, which bombed commercially. Driven into liquidation in the fall of 1980, the

company was forced to end its operation in May 1981. Conviction that patronage of the Lorton-Sanford train betokened a durable market capable of generating a useful surplus on direct costs, persuaded Amtrak two years later to revive the service on a thrice-weekly basis.

Critics still found more than one cause to berate Amtrak, particularly its alleged obsession with pampering the Northeast Corridor and the resultant failure, it was said, to develop some longer-haul routes which would give a better return on costs. There was discontent too, with Amtrak's arbitrary averaging-out of many costs over its various operations, instead of devising a system that would impute to each train as accurately as possible all the avoidable costs it individually incurred. Thus, for example, the high cost of keeping track in order for the 120mph New York-Washington "Metroliners" has to be borne equally by long-haul trains using the Northeast Corridor which are not equipped to exceed 79mph (the maximum permitted elsewhere in their itinerary – and throughout the Amtrak network – where infrastructure and locomotive equipment does not provide for continuous repetition of signal aspects in the engineer's cab).

The case for launching a new service, naturally, can be made to look falsely unsound if its prospective balance sheet is loaded with a share of Amtrak's total train operating costs that are quite irrelevant to its introduction. Some analysts argue that a more realistic, up-to-date accounting approach would show some possible new services as better financial prospects than one or two currently operated. Equally vulnerable to attack is the Amtrak method which apportions total on-train catering costs to services on the basis of their revenue: thus the expenses on a long-haul train serving main meals and expensive cocktails come out grossly overrated, and conversely those of the well-staffed "Metroliner," say, dealing chiefly in snacks and cheaper drinks,

absurdly undervalued.

But in 1985 Amtrak would be driven to a fundamental reappraisal of its accounting. Unless Congress again frustrated anything but minor surgery, the national passenger train operator was facing the most threatening assault yet on its finances – and even its existence. For the Budget proposals drafted by the Office of Management & Budget following the Reagan re-election included a proposal to end all Amtrak subsidies in their swingeing cuts to reduce the massive national deficit.

This blow coincided with a sharp setback for hopes of creating high-speed rail passenger service in other populated intercity corridors as well as the Northeast. The Department of Transportation and Congress had backed a study of the case for developing faster travel on the existing tracks of several corridors in the late 1970s. Impatient with the negative findings that emerged from this exercise, a number of states, particularly in the Midwest, began to consider ways and means of creating brand-new, high-speed railways between their key cities

under their own auspices – but hopefully not with their taxpayers' dollars, or at least with only marginal call on state funds. The models, naturally, were Japan's "Bullet Train" Shinkansen and, from the fall of 1981, France's first and immediately profitable 170mph TGV route between Paris and Lyons.

Another state in the forefront of high-speed aspirants was California. Its San Francisco-Los Angeles-San Diego corridor, with a population at least three times as numerous as the Northeast's, looked particularly promising territory. So in the spring of 1981 the American High Speed Rail Corporation (AHSRC) was set up with ex-Amtrak President Alan S Boyd as its Chairman to promote construction of an electrified 113-mile, 160mph Japanese-style line between Los Angeles, its airport and San Diego. A few months later AHSRC got an extraordinary fillip when an 83-year-old Japanese industrialist turned philanthropist, Ryoichi Sasagawa, put up $5 million of his own fortune to dispatch to California a Japanese engineering team. They arrived to execute comprehensive planning studies, carrying in

their baggage promises of $800 million in Japanese investment funds toward the estimated $2 billion-plus cost of constructing and equipping the line.

But as the 1980s unfolded, and though the enterprise looked from some angles to be firming in purpose with the appointments of project managers, banking advisers and engineering consultants, it was turning sour in other respects. A powerful faction in the state attacked the schemes, bonding to Japanese technology, without any detailed consideration of the high-speed systems now operationally proved in Europe. Environmentalists were roused. Above all there was an unanswered question: would AHSRC raise anything like the $1.5 billion of capital it intended to seek in the US? On this last count it fell at the very first hurdle. Shortly before 1984 closed it had to announce failure to come up with even the $50 million needed to start land acquisition moves along the railroad's prospective route. After this the project seemed, at least for the immediate future, to be moribund.

Of the other corridor schemes canvassed, the one with the most going for it looked to be a proposal to revamp and resignal an existing route between Chicago and Detroit for 125mph or slightly faster travel by trains based on the design of British Rail's HST. The HST, embodying the fruits of the British system's exhaustive scientific research into running gear design for high speed on orthodox track, is a streamlined, reversible train-set with a lightweight 2,250hp diesel-electric locomotive at each end. At the cost of some curve realignment, general track strengthening, and also some signaling adjustments, the British have been able to run HST services over distances of up to 250 miles at overall average speeds of more than 90mph, but without exceeding 125mph – and all on existing infrastructure, amid the rest of the system's passenger and freight traffic. Something similar, it has been calculated, could be achieved between Detroit and Chicago at only a third to half

Below: Tracked inter-city transport of tomorrow? Transrapid 06, passenger-carrying test train of the German Maglev system, bidding for a Los Angeles-Las Vegas link, on its elevated test track in the Emsland area of N. Germany.

the capital cost of building a new high-speed line. Bechtel is heavily involved in this attempt to implant British technology in the US.

The French, who have set up a company in the US to market their TGV technology, had their sights chiefly on Texas, where private interests have grouped to try for a high-speed rail link between Houston and Dallas; and on Florida, which in the spring of 1984 set up a High Speed Rail Corporation to oversee initial moves for a line between Miami, Orlando, and Tampa, although in 1986 the Corporation signed an exclusive agreement with the Bombardier company.

The other corridors where matters had progressed beyond pure ambition in 1984 were Chicago-Milwaukee-Minneapolis/St Paul and Los Angeles-Las Vegas. In both instances the spotlight is on the Maglev – magnetic levitation – system developed by the Transrapid consortium of West German industry, and which is naturally being promoted in the US by Budd, since Budd is now owned by a major in the West German Transrapid partnership, Thyssen-Henschel. Transrapid aims for top speed of 250mph with its system, in which a train, linear-motor driven and levitated on an air-cushion by the effect of powerful electromagnets in opposition, rides over an elevated guideway.

Ohio once looked purposefully bent in the direction of a high-speed railroad interconnecting Cleveland, Columbus, Detroit, Pittsburgh, and Toledo, but in a 1982 referendum voters rejected the raising of a sales tax to fund further development. In 1986 consideration was being given to a new route, Cleveland-Columbus-Cincinnatti, with a top speed of 165 mph.

Nevertheless, the California fiasco must have thrown a shadow on these other projects and their chances of attracting finance. That shadow will surely have deepened with the reelected Reagan Administration's budgetary proposals rendering even more remote any possibility of Federal aid for high-speed railway startup.

8
THE RAILROADS OF CANADA

In one respect Canada is unique among the great railroading nations. No other country has a state-owned and a privately-owned system in competition countrywide. The state-owned enterprise is CN Rail, the biggest component of Canadian National, whose other interests include trucking, telecommunications, mineral and petroleum resource development, coastal shipping, and, of course, the Grand Trunk collection of US railroads discussed in a preceding chapter. Its private enterprise rival, CP Rail, is part of the bigger Canadian Pacific conglomerate, which numbers international air and shipping lines among its businesses, as well as telecommunications, trucking, oil, gas, mining, iron and steel, forestry, agriculture, and real estate. CP Rail contributes less than a fifth of total Canadian Pacific income.

In the past 25 years Canadian railroading has undergone just as much vital change as that of the US. The first critical event was an Act of 1967 which, giving a lead to the US, deregulated freight transport – but with one outstanding exception, of which more in a moment. The railroads were freed from the straitjacket of standard, published rates for every commodity and could now market-price. Equally important was the ability to enter into long-term contracts with assurances that the deals struck amply provided for the renewal of existing assets or the creation of new stock that might be necessary to deal competently with the traffic.

In mid-century the long-haul passenger business was in the same disarray as the US railroads. CP Rail managed to extricate itself from most of its passenger operation by the 1960s, but CN Rail made a last attempt to reverse the downward trend in this sector by taking on United Aircraft's adventurous Turbotrains, by purchasing and refurbishing secondhand US streamliner equipment, and by image-revamping and bold marketing schemes. Sadly, discounted fares failed to generate enough new traffic to cover increased cost or equipment depreciation, and in the early 1970s CN Rail had to plead for relief from losses which had become intolerable, despite the Government's coverage of 80 percent of the deficit on any service it insisted must be maintained. In 1978 the Federal Government followed the US Amtrak pattern and transferred intercity passenger service management and marketing to a Government-funded agency, VIA Rail, which is considered later.

That same year, 1978, a Capital Revision Act transformed CN Rail's finances. For 20 successive years up to 1975 CN Rail had operated at an overall loss, partly because it was forced to pay a fixed rate of interest on money borrowed from the Government; if it did make a profit, any surplus had to be handed over to the Government, so that it was reliant on Federal benevolence for its capital investment. The 1978 legislation translated some $800 million of CN Rail accumulated debt into Government stock and reduced the dividend payable to 20 percent of CN Rail profits. In effect, the Government became an equity shareholder, taking a return on its investment that reflected CN Rail performance from year to year, not a fixed sum irrespective of whether CN Rail results were good or bad. At the same time,

Right: Canadian National serves the Cardinal River mine at Luscar, Alberta.

Left: CP Rail grain train crosses Canada's longest (5,328ft) and highest (314ft) rail bridge at Lethbridge, Alberta.

public funding for CN Rail investment was terminated. The railroad now has to generate all it needs by its own good housekeeping or by borrowing on the open market.

One major grievance still angered both railroads – the ludicrously uneconomic rate at which they were compelled to transport grain. Back in 1897 the Government of the day legislated to peg all rates for the movement of grain so as to stimulate exports, under what was known as the Crow's Nest agreement because it was concerned with transport through the Rockies pass of that name. By the 1970s the Crow grain rates had seen no adjustment since 1925, so that by then it was costing about 50 percent more to mail a letter from the prairies to a Pacific port than to rail a bushel of grain. The railroads' only redress was that the Government was undertaking the supply of new grain hoppers at no cost and also underwriting the maintenance of branch lines retained exclusively for collection of export grain. In 1978 these supports still left CN Rail and CP Rail together $175 million short of the full $354 million cost of moving that year's 21 million tons of railborne grain to the ports.

By the late 1970s Crow rates had become a disincentive to exports, the opposite of their original purpose. The railroads were obviously not prepared to invest in increased operating capacity to move the grain, nor was there any inducement to expand transshipment facilities at the ports. Rail handling capacity was also constricted because the Government's provision of new hoppers was not generous enough to obviate the use of quite unsuitable boxcars for a good deal of the grain traffic. The net result was that the railroads could not shift more than 60 percent of the grain offered for export; consequently, despite the eager world appetite for Canadian grain, many farmers were abandoning grain production altogether – analysts reckoned that at least 25 million acres were being left fallow.

Another absurdity was Crow's discouragement of any moves to make grain transport more efficient, by coaxing producers to load at a smaller number of sophisticated road-rail transshipment terminals. That would allow formation of economic full trainloads at source, as opposed to part-trains which had to be concentrated into full trains elsewhere at avoidable marshaling costs. Furthermore, compression of the grain input into fewer, bigger-scale terminals would allow elimination of some branch lines for a valuable reduction in upkeep and operational expenses.

After years of harrying on the Crow issue by both big railroads, the Govern-ment acted in 1983. It had at last awoken to the implications of the two systems' deferral of investment in their transcontinental operating capacity for Canada's other rich export trades in coal and minerals, above all to Japan. Legislation enacted in November 1983 offered CN and CP Rail an immediate and substantial grain transport subsidy totaling $658.6 million a year, over and above continuing Government commitments to fund both new hopper car construction and Prairie branch upkeep at a total outlay of over $300 million a year, pending a phasing-out of the infamous Crow rates. For their part, CN and CP Rail were required to guarantee annual rates both of forward investment and of grain movement to the ports.

At that, CP Rail knocked the chocks away from the climactic scheme in its program of capacity enlargement at the western end of its transcontinental route, on which it had already spent more than $300 million since 1976. Nothing less than the boring of two new single-track tunnels aggregating ten miles in length through the Rogers Pass area of the Selkirk Mountains would be put in hand, at a cost of at least $600 million. Considering the relationship of the rail system in revenue terms to the gross of all Canadian Pacific activity, this figure was striking testimony to private enterprise's valuation of railroading as a rewarding business in the concluding decades of the 20th century.

CP Rail's 625 miles of transcontinental route between Calgary and Vancouver is roughly 80 percent single track; and that 80 percent is arguably the busiest single-track trunk line in the world. Not in terms of numbers of trains daily, which is no more than 11 to 15 (at most) each way per 24 hours, but on a tonnage basis, which was as high as 55 million in 1980 – more than twice the total in 1970 – though the

Right: A unit train of British Columbia coal for Japan winds over Stoney Creek bridge, en route to Roberts Bank for shipment.

recession dipped the gross in 1981-82; that naturally solidified CP's decision to keep the Rogers Pass tunnel project on the back burner until the Crow grain rate burden was lifted.

Export grain from the Prairies accounts for about 20 percent of the traffic moving west of Calgary. Other important components are export shipments of potash from Saskatchewan, sulfur and petrochemicals from Alberta, and huge tonnages of Japan-bound coal from the mines on the western slopes of the Rocky Mountains in British Columbia, making a 693-mile run to the Roberts Bank shipment port, about 20 miles south of Vancouver.

These coal trains are operated like a conveyor belt, on what the British tag the "Merry-Go-Round" principle. At both pithead, where the trains are loaded from overhead silos, and at port, the rail layout is a continuous loop, so that either for loading or for discharge there is no need to break up a train into individual cars. Consequently the operation is based on the continuous circuiting of intact trains between coalfield and Roberts Bank. At the pithead, moreover, trains are loaded on the move, thanks to the fitting of diesel locomotives with a slow-speed device that enables them to inch their trains through the overhead bunker installation at an unvarying 0.5mph.

Loading to a gross of as much as 14,000 tonnes, these coal trains are the heaviest loads in CP Rail's mountain territory. The first stage of their haul is a 220-mile descent from the coalfield to the CP trunk route at Golden, where their traction undergoes a marked change. A maximum-weight train will have four 3,000hp SD-40 diesels hooked up front, four 3,000hp "slave" locomotives, Locotrol-controlled, inserted in pairs at suitable mid-train intervals and four more 3,000hp units backed up to its rear as helpers. This super-power is essential because

in its 100 or so miles from Lake Louise to the present Connaught Tunnel below Rogers Pass, CP Rail's transcontinental route confronts loaded trains with fearsome gradients. There are stretches as steep as 2.6 percent in the railroad's grapple with the mountains before it reaches Golden, but thereafter comes a long section at this pitch in the 20.9 miles from Rogers to Stoney Creek – the notorious Beaver Hill, with the 9,492ft peak of Mount Macdonald looming ahead, which carries the line up to the mouth of Connaught Tunnel.

Experts forecast that if the world clambers out of its general economic recession this stretch of CP Rail trunk route will need to process 20 trains each way daily by 1990, and be capable of handling up to 50 percent more tonnage. As things stand that would be impossible. Even with the 36,000hp punch of 2 diesel locomotives, a maximum-load coal train cannot better 20mph on the 2.6 percent grades, which means that it is in lengthy occupation of the single-sections, reducing the capacity to process trains in the reverse direction. Furthermore, eastbound paths must also be reserved for the return of helper locomotives to the foot of the climb. Neither increase of diesel power nor electrification – which CP Rail has carefully studied – would solve the problem, because on gradients of this ferocity it is coupler strength

which dictates the permissible length and weight of train, not the ultimate possibilities in maximum tractive effort (which is the reason, of course, for the mid-train marshaling of "slave" locomotives).

The only course open to CP Rail is construction of an additional track for loaded westbound trains that bypasses the most severely graded sections of the route. It has been pursuing this course since 1976, with the aim of lowering the maximum gradient in the westbound direction to 1 percent. In formidably difficult environmental conditions three new stretches of deviation track have already been completed, together totaling 21 route miles, between Calgary and Vancouver. Under way in 1984 was the biggest scheme of all, the construction of 21 miles of new line bypassing Beaver Hill on a steady 1 percent grade, and threading the Selkirk Mountains in two new tunnels, one a 1-mile bore, the other 9 miles long. The present Connaught Tunnel route will remain for the exclusive use of eastbound traffic.

In both tunnels the track foundation will be, not conventional ties and ballast, but a continuous concrete slab, to which the rails are directly fastened. This is a British system, devised to reduce greatly the track maintenance work needed where conditions are difficult; its first cost is heavy, but the later

savings have proved well worth the outlay. The longer Mount Macdonald tunnel will need one of the most elaborate and powerful ventilating systems yet installed in a rail bore, because of the effort the diesels of each climbing train will be putting out. This will be arranged to cleanse the eastern half of the tunnel once a train is past halfway, so that it will be feasible to work a train through once every half-hour.

Completion of the deviation will secure the 50 percent extra annual tonnage capacity even though the daily maximum throughput of trains is lifted by a smaller amount. At present the maximum load of freights other than coal hauls is around 10,500 tons. Hauled by six 3,000hp locomotives, they still need rear-end helpers to negotiate Beaver Hill, With the ruling gradient throughout held at 1 percent, helper service could be eliminated. A maximum load of up to 14,000 tons could be generalized for all westbound bulk commodity trains, which could be hauled throughout from Calgary to Vancouver by three head-on and two mid-train "slave" locomotives. Completion of the Rogers Pass deviation should make that possible by the end of 1989.

The Rogers Pass scheme is only one item in a huge capital investment and maintenance expenditure program announced by CP Rail throughout

Western Canada in the wake of the Crow rate decision. It includes spread of the latest in Centralized Traffic Control (CTC) systems and of other modern telecommunications, among them microwave links. On this last topic one should mention a CP Rail development on the Calgary-Vancouver sector that is as yet unique worldwide. To overcome problems of maintaining radio contact between dispatchers and train crews in the avalanche-prone area of the Illecillewaet River valley between Glacier and Revelstoke, just west of the Connaught Tunnel, CP Rail has abandoned the traditional pole lines. Transmission towers and 12ft-diameter reception-dishes have been installed to bounce the messages to and fro off the Anik B satellite, one that is in geosynchronous or stationary orbit in space.

In the mid-1980s CP was also at the mid-point of a 10-year program to update its diesel fleet. This entailed the rebuilding and modification of over 400 existing units at a cost of $48 million, the retirement of some 300 thoroughly outdated units and the purchase of up to 160 new units at a cost of around $162 million. Up to 1984, new buying was focussed principally on the General Motors EMD 3,000hp Type SD40-2 six-axle locomotive.

For CN Rail, too, double-tracking of more of its main line in western Cana-

Above left: a heavy mixed freight of grain and potash in the mountain section of the Calgary-Vancouver route. Note the radio-controlled "slave" locomotives mid-train.

Above: A CN unit train of export coal arrives at the new Ridley Island shipment terminal, British Columbia.

da has become a 1980s priority to cater for expanding world demand for Canadian grain, sulfur, coal, potash, and forest products. The latest refinements in computer-based CTC, by obtaining more precise regulation of movements through single-line sections, has reduced the amount of essential double-tracking needed to cope with today's record traffic compared with the mileage that would have had to be widened a decade or so ago. Nevertheless, CN Rail did establish Western Canada's longest continuous stretch of double track – 74 miles from Henry House, Alberta, through the Rocky Mountains' Yellowhead Pass to Valemount, British Columbia, on the trunk route from Edmonton to the Pacific Coast – in the early 1980s.

This is the vital CN Rail throat in Western Canada. At Red Pass Junction, 44 miles west of Jasper on the border between Alberta and British Columbia, is the convergence of CN Rail's north line from the port of Prince Rupert and its main line from Vancouver to Edmonton; and here trains of

Above: A CN unit train of sulfur threads Fraser Canyon, British Columbia.

Above right: Double-tracking in progress on Canadian National's trunk route east of Jasper, Alberta.

Below: CN lays concrete ties west of Kamloops, British Columbia.

forestry products from the north mingle with imports, including Japanese cars, heading east from Vancouver and the westbound tide of unit trains bearing coal, sulfur, potash, and grain. Like CP Rail's, these CN Rail shipment trains are mile-long rakes grossing up to at least 13,000 tons.

British Columbia north line through Prince George to Prince Rupert is set to triple its traffic at least by 1990, largely because of the creation of a huge new and highly mechanized coal and grain shipment port at Ridley Island, near Prince Rupert. A prime source of the coal is the Tumbler Ridge field in the Selkirk mountains to the northeast of the province, whence the tonnage is ferried to the CN Rail line by Canada's first high-voltage AC-electrified railway, the newly-built Tumbler Ridge branch of British Columbia Rail, to be described later.

Consequently CN Rail, having already laid out over $550 million between 1974 and 1982 to expand its operating capacity in the west of Canada, reacted to the Western Grain

Transportation Act which solved the Crow problem by budgeting almost $340 million of fresh investment in this territory for 1983, out of a total of $492 million scheduled for its network as a whole. Sustained annual expenditure at that level would by 1987 see CN Rail with more than a third of its 1,561 miles of trunk from Winnipeg to Vancouver to double track, 210 miles of it between Winnipeg and Edmonton, and 392 miles between Edmonton and Vancouver; with sophisticated dispatching and signaling systems in place throughout the area; and also with

important improvements completed at its Vancouver, Kamloops, Jasper, Edmonton, and Winnipeg terminals. Winnipeg developments include the planned introduction of robot switching locomotives at the city's Symington yard.

CN Rail has been a North American front-runner in the mechanization of track maintenance and track renewal. It was the first to adopt European concepts of compact, multi-machine train-sets for one-pass replacement of old track with new continuously-welded rail assemblies. Its P-811 track

renewal train removes existing rail and wooden ties, places new concrete ties in position, then threads welded rail along them ready for fastening, all at a rate of up to 2 miles a day. Incidentally, CN Rail was also one of the first systems in the continent to disconcert the timber industry by trying more costly but more durable concrete ties, which help to conserve the integrity of the track's geometry. It is now the major concrete tie user in North America.

In recent years CN Rail has bought a proportion of its line-haul diesel locomotives from the Canadian builder, Bombardier-MLW, as well as GM-EMD models. The most powerful units produced by this company – and employed by CP as well as CN Rail – are the six-axle 3,000hp M630 and 3,600hp M636, which are updated versions of the Alco 630 and 636 models. These were the last high-power models introduced in the US by Alco Products before that company sold its engineering designs and worldwide locomotive licensing agreements to its Canadian subsidiary, Montreal Locomotive Works, in 1969; the latter is now Bombardier-MLW. The most recent Bombardier-MLW model for CN Rail is a 3,200hp Type HR616 Co-Co with a unique wide, or cowl-type, body that is tapered inward at the rear of the cab, and which has a special air-ducting system, all designed for greater protection against the ingress of snow. From GM-EMD's high-power line CN Rail

has, like its rival, lately bought the SD40-2, but fitted with CN Rail's own design of so-called "comfort" cab. In 1984, however, CN placed orders for 29 3,500hp Type SD-50 Co-Cos from this manufacturer and late in the year it was to be the first Canadian recipient of four locomotives powered by GM-EMD's new 16-cylinder 710G-3 engine.

CN Rail bent to the general economic recession at the start of the 1980s and dipped briefly into a $43.3 million net loss in 1982, but otherwise it has never looked back since its successive release from the travails of passenger operation and from financial bondage to the

state. Its record of steady annual profit, 1982 alone excluded since the 1978 reconstruction of its finances, is an impressive achievement, recollecting the years of remorseless deficit which went before.

Deregulation has stiffened the sinews of both CN and CP Rail. As already recounted, Canada took this step more than a decade earlier than the US, though the response of its two major railroads was fairly supine until they were galvanized by the mid-1970s inflation of their costs following the oil price explosion. That roused them to discriminate in favor of high-volume business, shake off traditional across-the-board approaches to pricing, negotiate rates on a shipper-by-shipper basis, and enthrone modern marketing expertise at the right hand of top management. One should add that CN Rail's adoption of the same hardnosed, profit-centered attitudes as free-enterprise CP Rail owed a great deal to its acquisition of a forceful new Chief

Right: CN's MacMillan freight yard, Toronto.

Below: CN's Monport intermodal yard, Montreal.

Executive in 1974.

Of Canada's other railroads, BC Rail was the one commanding most attention in the mid-1980s. Until 1984 the railroad was integrated in the British Columbia Railway Co., a Crown corporation wholly owned by the province, but in a financial reorganization designed to reduce the railroad's debt burden it has now been reconstituted as a separate subsidiary of the corporation. Its 1,261-mile system runs from a waterfront terminal at North Vancouver northward to Prince George, Fort St John, and Fort Nelson.

BC Rail's current significance comes from its installation of Canada's first high-voltage AC rail electrification. The stimulus was the $2 billion development of British Columbia's northeastern coalfield, in the area between Prince George and Fort St John, which was launched in 1981 when protracted negotiations were sealed in contracts for the long-term supply of Japanese steel mills by two major British Columbia coal-mining concerns. With the new Ridley Island deep-sea bulk-loading terminal the prospective point of coal shipment, BC Rail would obviously be a vital link in the transportation scheme. Its main line passed within 100 miles of the Tumbler Ridge mine site; and at Prince George that main line interchanged with CN Rail's BC North route, offering direct access to Ridley Island.

Previously BC Rail had been chiefly dependent for its income on cyclical forestry traffic. The Japanese coal would not only more than double the railroad's annual tonnage but inject a great deal more stability into its financial performance. Consequently the provincial government needed little persuasion to back the $455 million construction of a new 80-mile Tumbler Ridge branch to the coalfield. Begun late in 1981, it was finished a month ahead of schedule in November 1983 – no mean achievement, considering the ferocious winter conditions in the region, plus the project's need of two major tunnels, one 5.6 and the other 3.8 miles long.

BC Rail had not at first contemplated electrification but, as building of the branch got under way, some substantial capital-cost as well as operating cost savings of such a traction course emerged. Installation costs would be tempered by the fact that the 230kV hydro-electric power lines were already strung up to the Tumbler Ridge mines; in addition, both Federal and provincial government contributions to the capital cost were on offer to enterprises that employed a renewable source of energy. Use of electric traction would also save the cost of equipping the two main tunnels with powerful, expensive ventilating plant to disperse the fumes of straining diesel engines.

So the whole Tumbler Ridge branch was electrified at 50kV 60Hz, only the fourth instance thus far in the world of a resort to so high a voltage (the benefit of 50kV, by comparison with the more commonly-used 25kV, is its need of fewer sub-stations to feed the traction

current wires, yet without risk of the current's power dropping to an unsatisfactory value at the extra distance from each supply point). The branch's seven Type GF6C 4,400kW Co-Co electric locomotives were built by General Motors of Canada, but their electrical equipment was designed and mostly built by ASEA, the Swedish electrical giant which conceived Amtrak's AEM-7 Bo-Bo for the US Northeast Corridor. The BC Rail locomotives, like the AEM-7s, embody the thyristor, stepless control of traction motors in which ASEA was one of the first electric traction firms in the world to specialize.

Only a third of the 450-mile haul from the Tumbler Ridge pithead to Ridley Island is on BC Rail metals, so CN Rail, which built the entire 913-strong fleet of coal hoppers for the project, retains ownership of three-quarters of them. They are operated in 98-car trains grossing 13,000 tons fully loaded, which set off from Tumbler Ridge fronted by two of the new electrics (which normally work in couples, leaving one on standby). At Tacheeda, the branch's junction with the BC Rail main line, CN Rail diesels take over for the remainder of the transit to Ridley Island, crewed by BC Rail men as far as the convergence with BC Rail at Prince George. On the final stretch from Prince George to Ridley Island, the crews are employees of CN Rail.

This is another "Merry-Go-Round"-type exercise. Both at Tumbler Ridge and Ridley Island the terminal track layouts are circular, so that trains need no uncoupling during loading and discharge. The full operating plan has nine 98-car trains in continuous circuit between mines and port, each of them on a 75-hour schedule for the 900-mile round trip, including loading and discharge time.

Even before inauguration of the Tumbler Ridge-Ridley Island coal run, BC Rail's economy had become buoyant, producing in 1982 the highest net revenue in the railroad's history, then triumphantly doubling surplus in 1983, much more through streamlined

operating methods and plant modernization than because of rising traffic. That puts it in good stead to respond to fresh heavy industrial development in the province. The opening up – again for Asian markets – of anthracite mines in northwestern British Columbia to complement the bituminous coal output of Tumbler Ridge, and their connection by new rail to a transshipment development at Stewart, at the head of the Portland Canal, is one serious possibility.

At the start of the 1980s BC Rail bought a dozen GM-EMD SD40-2 Co-Cos, but otherwise it is a stronghold of basically Alco models by Bombardier-MLW. Passenger service is offered over the 320 miles between North Vancouver and Prince George, but makes a minimal 1 percent contribution to BC Rail income. It is furnished by Budd RDC railcars, which in the early 1980s were betraying the effects of 25 years' daily grinding up a route beset with a 2.5 percent ruling gradient, and which was in places sustained for a considerable distance. But from 1982 a

thorough refurbishing, including installation of new engines and transmissions, was progressively put in hand on the railroad's own six RDCs and subsequently extended to three further cars taken over on a 100-year lease from the Philadelphia, US, transport authority in 1983.

In piquant contrast to its latter-day sophistication, which besides AC electrification includes a radio-controlled, computer-assisted traffic control system that has excited foreign interest (see Chapter 5), BC Rail delights the sentimentalists by cherishing former Canadian Pacific "Royal Hudson" 4-6-4 No 2860 in working order – and in a gleaming rendition of the engine's regal maroon and black livery in its prime. In summer it is used to work a nine-car train, including an open-sided observation car, over the 40 miles fringing the Howe Sound between North Vancouver and Squamish – a stirring scenic as well as nostalgic experience, though the mountain grandeur is still more awesome north of Squamish.

To the east, the passenger fleet of

Far left: BE Rail freight train headed by SD40-2s skirts Seton Lake, near Lillooet.

Left: One of BC Rail's new 50kV ac electric locomotives, built by GM and employing electric traction technology by ASEA of Sweden.

Above: On the newly-electrified Tumbler Ridge branch, a pair of Type GF8C 4400kW locomotives head a 98-car coal train.

Below: VIA tilt-body LRC train crosses the Richelieu river at Beloeil, Quebec, east of Montreal.

another provincial railway, the Ontario Northland, was set for a spectacular infusion of new equipment by early 1986. The new ingredient is a long-haul version of the aluminum-bodied bilevel commuter cars built by Hawker Siddeley Canada – whose passenger car-building business is now under the aegis of Can Car Rail at Thunder Bay (Ontario) – or Government of Ontario (GO) Transit.

Hawker Siddeley entertained hope of a long-haul buyer when it drafted its bilevel design. For that reason it rejected the "gallery" interior format of other North American commuter bilevels, such as the C&NW locomotive-hauled and ICG "Highliner" electric mus in the Chicago region, in which there is air space from central gangway floor to roof and the upstairs seating is on shelves on each side-wall. Between trucks, which have air suspension, the Canadian car-body is sunk close to rail level, creating height within the loading gauge sufficient for each level to be fully enclosed as a separated storey. The distinctive external feature of these bilevels is their lozenge-shaped ends, where the interior is single-storey at an othodox floor level; besides allowing space for a pantograph should any system consider the design as suitable for an electric mu format, this is claimed to package a bilevel train into a more effective aerodynamic outline than a conventional car-body shape.

Ontario Northland, a component of the multi-modal Ontario Northland Transportation Commission's operations, is a 574-mile system at the eastern rim of the province, running from North Bay, where it is intersected by CN and CP Rail routes westward from Ottawa, to Moosonee on James Bay, the southward-probing neck of Hudson Bay. Freight, chiefly lumber, pulp, newsprint, and ores, is the backbone of its business, but it runs two significant passenger services into and out of Toronto Union station, traveling 228 miles of CN Rail track between there and the fringe of its own territory at North Bay.

One of these, the "Northlander" from Toronto to Timmins, 487 miles distant, attracted attention in 1977 when Ontario Northland reequipped it with imported European material – four of the original Dutch/Swiss all first-class, diner-equipped "Trans-Europ Express" train-sets which had been discarded on their home ground when the spread of the continent's trunk route electrification made international electric working with locomotive-hauled cars more practicable than at the TEE scheme's inception. The Dutch/Swiss diesel electric TEE sets were operated across Europe as double-ended, permanently-coupled units, but their twin-engined, 2,000hp traction was bulked in what

was effectively a locomotive at one end. Never paragons of the European traction builder's art, these power cars did not take to their exile and in 1979 the railroad supplanted them with rebuilt FP7-A diesels from its own mainly GM-EMD locomotive fleet, which otherwise features SD40-2s, GP38-2s and GP-9s.

In line for the bilevels was the "Northland," a joint operation with CN Rail, including a VIA Rail sleeper, which takes the Ontario Northland route as far as Cochrane, then CN Rail tracks from there to Kapuskasing (as well as from Toronto to North Bay, of course). The order was for eight cars, at a cost of roundly $1.5 million apiece, and the bill has been covered by Ontario's Ministry of Northern Affairs; development of the design has been subsidized by the Federal Department of Regional Industrial Expansion.

Destined for display at Expo 86, Vancouver's summer 1986 world's fair, before they were entrusted to Ontario Northland, the bilevels were to be employed as three-car sets; two in each set would be combination coach-sleepers, with reclining chairs on the upper deck and roomettes, and bedrooms on the lower, while the third would be a

Below: Cutaway impression of a new bi-level car under construction for Ontario Northland, delivered in 1986.

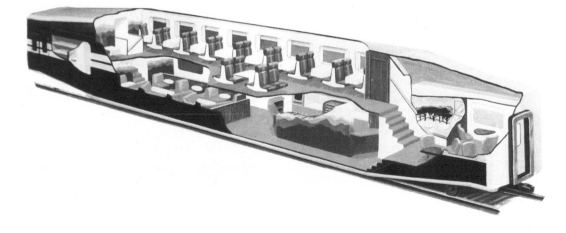

so-called "activity" car with a bar-lounge above and a diner and snack bar below. To complement the electrically-powered bilevels, Ontario Northland would have to create some auxiliary electricity generator cars, as its FP7-A diesels can only feed steamheated cars. The new bilevels would certainly be heavyweights; the GO Transit commuter parents of the design weigh only 54 tons apiece, but with their more compendious equipment each long-haul version was expected to scale 70-80 tons, perpetuation of the GO Transit design's extruded aluminum frame and aluminum bodyside construction not withstanding.

What are probably Canada's heaviest passenger trains are a hallmark of the Algoma Central Railway, a 322-mile line whose chief function is to lift forestry products and ore out of the north of the province; the line runs south from Hearst to Sault Ste Marie on Lake Superior, interchanging with both CN and CP Rail en route. Algoma Central offers a regular passenger service throughout its length, but the eyecatching passenger operation is its summer Agawa Canyon day tour, which the railroad promotes intensively throughout the midwestern US as well as in Canada, and which has attracted more than 100,000 clients in a season. It frequently calls for a consist of 20 cars and has been known to demand as many as 27. Besides ex-CP Rail cars of late 1940s vintage, the Algoma Central fleet sports a number of ex-US streamliner cars, among them some former Central of Georgia and Illinois Central vehicles, and – particularly captivating – a quintet of onetime Southern Pacific articulated units, though in 1984 only three of these were in revenue employment. The locomotive roster is exclusively GM, Canadian-built and headed by three SD-40s, six SD40-2s and six GP38-2s (these last added to stock in 1981).

Ontario was the North American pioneer of state-operated commuter passenger transportation. In the 1940s and 1950s a stunning rate of residential growth inflated population to the east and west of Toronto by as much as 450 percent, and with it a rising tide of peak-hour travel that was choking the city's access highways. The rail alternative was both inadequate in provision and unappealing in quality. In 1962, therefore, the provincial government set up a study group to consider courses that would fend off an impending transportation crisis. Their solution, based on exhaustive engineering and social research throughout a 5,000 square-mile area covering all sides of the city and embracing a population of 2.8 million that might almost triple by the year 2000, was investment in a superior rail service, starting with a 41.5-mile route along the Lake Ontario shore from Oakville and Pickering.

The government accepted the conclusions in the spring of 1965 and Government of Ontario Transit, better known as GO Transit, was launched with a $24 million investment. Today GO Transit is an integrated bus and rail system with a combined annual ridership of some 23 million, catering for a

Above right: GM-EMD FP7, de-engined to serve as push-pull driving cab and train auxiliary power supply, fronts GO Transit train on Lakeshore line in east Toronto: traction comes from the pushing GP40-2 at rear.

Below: Upper floor of GO Transit bi-level.

territory of more than 3,000 square miles and a current population of around 4 million, and operating six rail routes centered on Toronto Union station over CN and CP Rail tracks. The trains are run by the two railroads with their own crews under contract to GO Transit, and to GO Transit specifications.

GO Transit opened its rail account with eight diesel locomotives, nine railcars, and 40 single-level cars. By 1984 this stock had swollen to 32 locomotives, 14 auxiliary power units (APUs), 121 single-level, and 151 of the distinctive and majestic bilevel cars mentioned in the account of Ontario Northland's bilevel development. In their original commuter format one of these cars seats as many as 162 – 54 on its lower, 72 on its upper deck and a total of 36 in the intermediate-floor sections above each deck. Their internal decor was as stylishly colorful as GO Transit's brilliant exterior scheme of green and white. In the early 1980s the bilevel stock was hoisted to 151 by a repeat order for 71 cars, completed in

101

1983 and expected to result in withdrawal of some single-level cars.

In the repeat order 15 cars were built as cabbed driving trailers, since many GO Transit operations are push-pull. Previously the driving-trailer function had to be formed by 11 of the APUs – GM-EMD FP-7 diesels stripped of their traction plant to serve as 600kW "hotel supplies" generators for train electrical equipment – which were additionally rebuilt for the job. For the rest, GO Transit power comprises six FP40H, eight GP40TC, and 18 GP40-2, all 3000hp GM products.

As the 1980s dawned, traffic on GO Transit's original Lakeshore line was reaching saturation point. To enlarge its capacity the provincial government initially contemplated and authorized electrification, resignaling and some additional tracking (the existing tracks have to be shared with CN Rail freight and VIA intercity passenger trains). However, second thoughts concluded the money would be more wisely spent in escaping the chronic wrangles over fair rental for use of CN or CP Rail right-of-way and operating by laying down new infrastructure owned and worked exclusively by the province. Ontario has no capital fixed assets to show for the $100 million it has already plowed into track, signaling, and station facilities.

GO Transit's development strategy is now founded on the spread of an Advanced Light Rail Transit (ALRT), 25kV AC-electrified and computer-controlled system conceived by Canada's Urban Transportation Development Corporation (UTDC). Light Rail Transit gets detailed discussion, so it will suffice to note here that the GO Transit plan envisages ALRT operation with articulated six-axle twin-car units, able to seat 124 and stand a further 86 passengers, fit for 75mph top speed, and arranged for mu operation in rakes of up to five twin-sets. The first phase of the ALRT project, launched in 1984, was tracking extensions of 15 and 20 miles, one at each end, on to the present Lakeshore route, with substitution of this by a new ALRT line throughout to follow at an as yet unspecified date. However, at the beginning of 1985, an election resulted in a new Provincial government. Six months later the new Transport minister cancelled the whole project. The explanation was that new Federal laws had opened up the national network to all provinces and therefore the GO-ALRT scheme was no longer necessary. The money to be saved was obviously also taken into consideration.

In the spring of 1985 Toronto opened, on a 4.4-mile route in the Scarborough area, an example of another UTDC concept, its Intermediate Capacity Transit System (ICTS). This is one of the first rail passenger systems in the Western World to introduce fare-paying customers to propulsion by electric linear induction motors. As its ICTS tag implies, the system is designed for attractively frequent service of urban routes with insufficient traffic volume to warrant a full Light Rail Transit, let alone a sophisticated metro. Hence it is worked by comparatively small cars, plying singly or in pairs, moving at close headway under the automatic control of a so-called "moving block" system known as Seltrac and devised by the West German signaling specialists, Standard Elektrik Lorenz. In essence, "moving block" substitutes for the geographically fixed track sectioning of traditional signaling a spacing that is fully mobile, adjusted to match the progress of adjacent trains, but yet securing the same predetermined distance between them as a fixed signaling system.

Linear propulsion also figures in the ALRT system which UTDC has been applying to a 13.3-mile route from downtown Vancouver to its suburb of New Westminster; a short demonstration section was ready in 1983, but public service was not expected until 1986. The Vancouver line was single cars and the same Seltrac automatic control as Toronto's Scarborough line, arranged to permit service at minimum

Above: A GP40TC of GO Transit heads bi-levels on the Richmond Hill line near downtown Toronto.

Left: SD40s wheel a Quebec North Shore & Labrador haul of ore down to Sept-Iles port.

one-minute headways between cars in the peak hours. In the center of the city the ALRT has taken over a former CP Rail tunnel; elsewhere it has been erected mostly on elevated concrete guideways.

Montreal and Toronto are the only Canadian cities with full metro networks, which are more conveniently treated in a later chapter considering North American metro advances in general. For the rest, Montreal's commuter needs are met by two residual services run over CN and CP Rail tracks, the former a vintage 2.7kV electric operation to Deux Montagnes, the latter a diesel locomotive-hauled working from the dishevelled pile that was once CP Rail's noble Windsor terminal in the city. After years of deterioration and recrimination from the two railroads over inadequate compensation for the obligatory maintenance of the services, which culminated in a CP Rail threat to abandon and hang the consequences, both were taken over in 1982 by the Montreal Urban Community Transport Commission (MUCTC – or CTCUM locally, where French rendition of the title is *de rigeur*). The traction and rolling stock of both has since been committed to long-overdue renovation, including external application of a pleasing MUCTC livery of white-lined, two-tone blue. The long-term future of these services is now enmeshed in a plan drafted by a Quebec planning task force, COTREM, to create a six-route Montreal Regional Express Metro, on the model of Paris' cross-city, main line scale RER system; but by 1984 this idea

had not advanced beyond the conceptual stage.

Finally, a glimpse of two Quebec-based railways which are among the most remarkable heavy-haul systems in the world. Both have been built since World War II, when the extent of the ore deposits in the northeast of the province was first fully appreciated.

Begun in 1950 by its then newly-formed owners, the Iron Ore Company of Canada (IOC), with shareholding support of several US steelmakers, the 356-mile main line of the Quebec, North Shore, & Labrador Railway runs from Schefferville south to Sept-Iles on the St Lawrence. Schefferville, the rail head for the Ungava ore tract in the Labrador peninsula, is just inside the Quebec border, but otherwise the northern half of the route is enclosed by Newfoundland. Within this section a 36-mile branch was run from Ross Bay westward to Labrador City in 1960.

IOC stopped mining in the Schefferville area in 1982, but still serves the railhead as there are no roads north of Sept-Iles. Mining is now concentrated in the Carol Lake area, at the extremity of the Labrador City branch. Despite the savagery of winter in the region, QNS&L functions all year round, though in winter it moves only processed – or "benefited" – ore in pellets, because of "raw" ore's propensity to freeze.

QNS&L has a stock of over 4,000 ore cars which it runs in loaded trains varying from 117 to no fewer than 240 cars in length; the latter trail about 1.6 miles behind their lead locomotives and can gross over 32,000 tons, while a

117-wagon train tots up to a healthy 14,000 tons. Normal power at the front end is three or four 3,000hp GM-EMD SD-40s from the railroad's 76 unit-strong fleet, but when a train is made up to 165 cars or more, mid-train helper units, radio-controlled by the Locotrol system from the lead locomotive, are added. The whole line is traffic-controlled by CTC from Sept-Iles.

To the west of QNS&L the 281-mile Cartier Railway, a subsidiary of US Steel, is a similar ore carrier, threading equally rugged country from mines and ore concentrators at Mount Wright, Fire Lake, and Lac Jeannine (near Gagnon) down to the St Lawrence at Port Cartier, 40 miles from Sept-Iles. The 193 miles from the waterfront to Lac Jeannine were built in 1958-60 and the 86-mile Mount Wright branch was added in the early 1970s.

Cartier claims to have found mammoth trains too costly to work – it has experimented with consists of up to 298 of its rotary-dump hoppers – and has settled for 150-car trains with three 3,600hp diesels, one a Locotrol-controlled rear-end helper, as the optimal summer format. One of these can lift 14,000 tons of ore in a single movement. In winter, however, the railway prudently reduces the maximum loading to 90 cars; then ambient temperature can plummet to −40°C. These summer and winter train sizes have been proved the ideal match for the capacity of the mine loading and port discharge installations. All trains, incidentally, are manned by just two crewmen apiece; and none are tailed by a caboose. In recent years computer aids have been superimposed on Cartier's CTC. Despatching orders are transmitted to train crews by radio.

Cartier is basically Alco/MLW oriented in its motive power, though it does own seven 1,750hp GM-EMD units. The MLW fleet is headed by 24 M636 3,600hp units and 10 M630 3,000hp units.

9
OUTLOOK BRIGHTENS FOR CANADA'S VIA RAIL

At the end of 1976 the Canadian Government finally agreed to CN and CP Rail's clamor to be shot of losses on the passenger services which they were statutorily obliged to operate. Since legislation of 1967 the Government had shouldered 80 percent of their passenger deficits. Even so the two railroads together were over $50 million a year out of pocket on their passenger working.

In January 1977 VIA Rail Canada was set up under the wing of Canada's Transport Ministry. At first it was structured as a subsidiary of Federally-owned CN Rail, which had originated the VIA Rail brand-name in a last despairing revamp of CN passenger marketing in April 1976. But in April 1978 VIA was cut loose; and in October that year it took charge of CP as well as CN passenger services.

Since 1978 VIA has been one of Canada's 300 or so Crown Corporations. Funded by the Federal Government, its charge is to manage and market under the Transport Minister's direction all passenger services bar city metros, provincially sponsored commuter systems like GO Transit and Montreal's suburban workings, and the passenger activity of regional carriers Algoma Central, British Columbia, and Ontario Northland, which were discussed in Chapter 8. It has taken over the former CN and CP locomotives, railcars and other rolling stock deployed on services assumed by VIA, plus those services' train crews and station staff, and responsibility for all customer services, from reservations to publicity. Unlike Amtrak in the US, VIA owns no track, stations or – until the early 1980s, when it made a start on establishing a national chain of its own maintenance depots – even workshops.

Thus VIA has to contract with CN and CP for most of its back-up services as well as for day-to-day train operation.

The opening of VIA's account was superficially promising. True, there was some immediate rationalization of routes and services, notably off-season consolidation of the ex-CN "Super Continental" and ex-CP "Canadian" trans-continentals between Sudbury and Winnipeg and cancellation of the "Scotian" between Montreal and the Maritime provinces, but these had been anticipated. On the plus side, train ridership countrywide climbed 41 percent between 1977 and 1981 in response to VIA's lively and innovative marketing. The new strength was chiefly in the eastern, 727-mile Quebec City-Windsor corridor, threading the cities of London, Montreal, Ottawa, Sarnia, and Toronto, where VIA bit into the business travel market with a premium-fare "VIA-1" offer packaging pre-reserved first-class accommodation and superior on-train meal service. Elsewhere traffic was also boosted by imaginative pricing and marketing of CN and CP rail services as an integral national network for the first time, and by the 1980 commissioning of a computerized reservation and ticket system, Reservia, evolved jointly with another Crown Corporation, Air Canada.

At the same time Premier Trudeau's Liberal administration made a down-payment on pledges to support VIA with upgrading investment in the eastern corridor by authorizing series production of the LRC. This was a low-slung, aluminum alloy-bodied, high-

Right: The transcontinental "Canadian", including a dome car, crosses the Columbia River at Revelstoke, British Columbia.

Left: Montreal-Toronto LRC north of Lake Ontario at Napanee.

speed train-set developed by a Canadian industrial consortium and built by Bombardier-MLW, of which a prototype had been on trial since the mid-1970s. Designed for a maximum speed of 125mph on the straight, the LRC was also equipped to negotiate curvature faster than orthodox equipment.

Its passenger cars – but not its 102-ton, 2,600hp, Alco 251-engined B-B diesel-electric locomotive – were equipped with automatic body-tilting: that is, a system in which an accelerometer automatically sensed and measured rising lateral *g*, or centrifugal force, as a car entered a curve, and its findings were instantaneously translated by electronics into commands of a mechanism that added an appropriate degree of additional, artificial banking to the car body throughout its negotiation of the bend. That way passengers should not be subjected to any more lateral *g* in an LRC than in a conventional car taking the curve maybe 20-30mph more slowly. The LRC acronym, incidentally, stood for a less-than-beguiling "Light, Rapid, Comfortable" tag: the train's progenitors were presumably unable to come up with any brighter inspiration that respected their Quebec province's linguistic obsessions by having an identical French connotation – *"Léger, Rapide, Confortable."*

Delivery of the initial order of 21 LRC locomotives and 50 passenger cars began in late 1981. But by then VIA was embroiled in financial crisis. In stark contrast to sanguine political hopes of the late 1970s that a rationalized passenger system, inventively marketed as one entity, would break-even one day, VIA was soaking up more taxpayers' dollars by the year. As against $231 million in 1979, VIA needed $441 million to top up its $160 million of fare revenue in 1981 if its running costs were to be covered. Add to that capital investment bills to be footed by the Government and the full call on Federal money that year was $540 million. In the ensuing two years it was to exceed $580 million.

The snag was that VIA desperately needed more investment cash. The first LRC build was a trifling infusion of new equipment set against the 25-year age of 90 percent of VIA's fleet of second-hand CN and CP cars, over 800 of them; some, in fact, were third-hand acquisitions, as in its early 1960s drive to refound a viable passenger business CN bought and refurbished some discarded US streamliner equipment, including ex-Milwaukee full-length dome cars and ex-Reading and ex-Milwaukee observation saloons. Age was steadily aggravating both the cost and the difficulty of keeping these antiques in order: and their steam heating, terribly vulnerable to freeze-up failure in Canadian winters, was a serious deterrent to sales in the 1980s.

The solution imposed in mid-1981 by

Left: A typical VIA train of conventional equipment: elderly GM-EMD diesels and former CN or CP Rail cars.

Right: Section of VIA sleeper car arranged for day use.
Center: Same section set up for sleeping.

the Trudeau Government's then Transport Minister, Jean-Luc Pepin, was briefly: if you want more new trains, then enough services have to be cut to save at least $100 million a year in subsidy of your running costs to pay for them. VIA's founding legislation made no statutory provision for balanced Parliamentary discussion, or independent tribunal consideration of proposed changes in its operating network. The Transport Minister is VIA's sole judge and jury. So despite vociferous public protest, an order for 10 more LRC locomotives and 50 passenger cars was balanced in mid-November 1981 by enforced cutbacks that included total elimination of the "Super Continental" via Ottawa, Saskatoon, Edmonton, and Jasper to Vancouver, also of the overnight "Atlantic Limited" between Montreal and St John (New Brunswick), abandonment of seven VIA routes and drastic reduction of train frequency on four more. Worst treated were western Canada and the Maritime provinces: in Quebec and Ontario, the Government's electoral stronghold, VIA's Montreal-Ottawa, Montreal-Windsor, and Toronto-Windsor "Rapido" services were simultaneously intensified in frequency.

Pepin ignored a major factor inflating VIA's costs – its relationship with its CN and CP Rail track landlords. From the start VIA had been given no legislated authority to query the two railroads' billing for use of their infrastructure: and no obligation whatever was laid on the railroads to operate VIA trains with optimal economy. The formulae on which CN and CP Rail based their charges was never revealed in detail and had no statutory need to be: known only was the fact that each monthly statement quite unfairly sad-

Right: VIA diner.

107

dled VIA with a share of total costs incurred on each route (much of which would be unaffected if passenger trains were totally withdrawn) in addition to the "avoidable" expenses fully attributable to superimposition of passenger trains on the lines' freight operation. There were rural lines in Ontario and Manitoba where CN offloaded practically all costs on VIA even though passenger service consisted of a single car tacked on to a routine freight train! Worse yet, the railroads were quite free to hit VIA with a supplementary invoice at the end of each year claiming a handsome increment on the monthly amounts, purportedly for passenger train expenses overlooked or unforeseen during the previous 12 months. In 1981 these afterthoughts alone added up to $42 million.

For VIA 1982-83 were nervous years. The 1981 controversies helped to stunt and reverse business growth: from just over 8 million passenger journeys logged in 1981, the annual total had receded to 6.73 million by 1983's end. Summer loading of the surviving transcontinental, the "Canadian," to as many as 20 cars west of Calgary demonstrated rail's ongoing appeal as a grandstand for viewing the majestic mountain scenes, given attentive on-train service and astute promotion to offset the dated character of the train's equipment, which substantial interior refurbishing could not disguise. With salable fare levels covering at best a third of the "Canadian's" running costs with such elderly but elaborately-equipped cars, the "Canadian" was surviving on borrowed time. The same went for other long-haul services: and equally for the secondhand GM-EMD FPA4, FP7, and FP9 B-Bs constituting the greater part of the VIA traction fleet. At the end of 1989 the "Canadian" was discontinued.

In the Quebec-Windsor corridor, which generates over two-thirds of all VIA business, the LRCs made a chequered debut. First teething troubles delayed their entry into full public service until June 1982. Troublefree,

the LRCs earned rich compliments for their smooth and serene riding, but niggling malfunctions of various components persisted – one should qualify that by observing that at least the LRC was the first high-speed, tilt-body equipment anywhere in the world to pass proving muster for commitment to squadron service. These harassments limited their top speed to 80mph for a period in 1983, and in 1984 compelled VIA to immobilize the tilting apparatus completely. By the fall of that year remedied modifications by Bombardier gave hope that the system's frailties had been conclusively overcome. Nevertheless the LRCs' assignment to regular services on the Montreal-Toronto, Montreal-Ottawa, Montreal-Quebec, Ottawa-Toronto, and Toronto-Windsor routes featured such estimable performances as 4½ hour schedules for the 335-mile Montreal-Toronto run, inclusive of intermediate stops at Kingston and at the suburban railheads of Guildford (Toronto) and Dorval (Montreal).

VIA itself was doing its best to keep up a quality service at minimal cost. For instance, dinner menus were trimmed to offer just a two-entree option: but meals were still prepared on trains and there was no recourse to drab microwave oven processing of food pre-packaged on the ground, nor abandonment of decent china tableware and tablecloths. Laudable, too, was top VIA executives' readiness now and then to leave their desks, don a uniform and take a front-line turn at jobs like porterage, diner crew or ticket clerk to get a grassroots feel of staff problems and customer reactions.

But politicians could not be induced to reconsider some of the serious illogicalities hampering VIA that were beyond the corporation's power to change. What, for instance, was the sense of treating VIA financially as one homogeneous enterprise when it encompassed such vastly different activities as hopelessly lossmaking backwoods branch services which no politician would dare shut down, because

they catered for remote areas devoid of good roads: and at the other end of the scale, potentially viable intercity service in the Quebec-Windsor corridor, where VIA claimed 15 percent or more of the total travel market on at least two routes, Montreal-Toronto and Toronto-Windsor? Those shares were capable of increase if promises of 1976-77 to upgrade corridor infrastructure were implemented. As things stood, it was impossible to exploit an LRC's 125mph top speed. The ceiling had to be 95mph, and that only over short stretches, with 75mph the norm, because of curvature and signaling constraints, the existence of many grade crossings with roads, and VIA's enforced route-sharing with freight traffic.

From mid-1983, happily, some encouraging gleams temporarily pierced the mist cloaking VIA's future prospects. The event which mainly lightened the outlook was a Liberal cabinet reshuffle which shunted the flinty Jean-Luc Pepin to another post and appointed to his Transport Ministry chair Lloyd Axworthy. The newcomer soon revealed a more supportive attitude to VIA. It was necessary in the wake of Pepin's ruthless surgery, he told a Toronto audience early in 1984, "to restore confidence (in VIA), demonstrating a commitment to modernizing and improving." Anything from 300 to 600 new cars, he agreed, would be an inescapable VIA need by 1987-88.

Intention was soon translated into action. Additions to the VIA timetable were announced in 1984, the most notable a restoration of part of the onetime "Super Continental" itinerary in a new train named "Panorama" (a title once borne by a CP transcontinental) linking Winnipeg with Prince Rupert on the Pacific coast via Saskatoon, Edmonton, and Jasper. This would be launched in 1985 with a locomotive and four bilevel "Superliners" leased from Amtrak. It had already been surmised that VIA would vote for a bilevel format if and when it was allowed to reequip its long-haul trains, and the belief was reinforced

with the news that a Canadian-built long-haul bilevel design would soon exist as hardware on Ontario Northland, as noted in Chapter 8. Loan of existing Amtrak bilevels for public service would give Axworthy valuable scope to evaluate the pros and cons of this layout before reaching an investment decision.

The flow of hopeful news continued. Negotiations with CN and CP Rail seemed set to come up with a more realistic formula for the railroad's billing of VIA by 1984's end; and there was a hint that by the end of the decade the management of 80 or more major stations might have been handed over to VIA. Then, on top of VIA's commitment to a $300 million investment in its own rolling stock maintenance shops network-wide, Axworthy approved in August 1984 a $100 million start on rolling stock rehabilitation and renewal. Main items listed were 11 new GM or Bombardier-built locomotives; conversion to electrical auxiliary equipment powering of 83 long-haul cars; and experimental introduction of a two-axle railbus devised by Winnipeg Coach Sales on Manitoba branch lines.

Axworthy was ousted when Canada's general election in the late 1984 summer dealt his party a firm rejection. But the incoming Progressive Conservatives had campaigned on even more positive backing of VIA, with their leader, the new Premier Brian Mulroney, promising reinstatement of yet more routes (including the Montreal-St John "Atlantic"), renewal of VIA equipment, and revision of the VIA legislation to give the corporation a better-defined standing. Reversal of any of Axworthy's moves seemed improbable to most observers of the Canadian scene. Then in the face of 1984 came abrupt disillusion; not only was the new locomotive purchase and 83-car reconditioning called in question, but the maintenance depot scheme halted for reappraisal.

The LRCs were originally acquired within the framework of a prospectus that assumed both ideal performance

by the train-sets themselves and full redemption of political promises to rebuild corridor infrastructure as necessary to maximize use of the LRCs' 125mph capability. Both conditions realized, VIA envisaged schedules of 3 hours 40 minutes for the 335-mile Montreal-Toronto run, 2½ hours for Toronto-Windsor (224 miles), 1 hour from Montreal-Ottawa (112 miles), and 1¼ hours for Montreal-Quebec (155 miles). To overcome the problem that the corridor's double-track main lines were shared with freight, making it difficult to carve timetable paths for much faster LRCs that would not have them catch up slow-moving tonnage and be checked until it got out of the way, VIA recommended reorganizing the double track as two bi-directional single tracks, one for passenger, the other for freight. Both passenger and freight train movements either way were comparatively infrequent. Therefore, VIA argued, if each line were adequately equipped with passing loops and supervised throughout by modern, computer-based CTC, there should be no difficulty in smoothly processing either type of traffic on its dedicated line.

In 1983 VIA put in hand a $5 million study that reappraised this prospectus and projected potential business development against a wide range of investment options, from persistence with the make-do-and-mend that had been forced on so much VIA operations in the early 1980s to creation of new

Above: The comfortable interior of an LRC.

high-speed systems, whether steel-wheel-on-steel-rail or more exotic, such as Maglev. Its conclusion, presented to the Government early in 1984: a $2.1 billion conversion of existing railroad infrastructure between Montreal, Ottawa, and Toronto into a 160mph, French TGV-like electrified line, achieving 3 hours 10 minutes Montreal-Toronto and 1 hour 50 minutes Montreal-Quebec transits, would pay for itself within 25 years. If the project were launched immediately it could be finished for 1994 opening; and in that inaugural year, VIA's analysis concluded, it would pull in at least 7 million passengers, but by the second decade of the next century the gross should have risen to 14 million. At the same time the Windsor-Toronto and Montreal-Quebec routes should be made fit for 100mph use by diesel trains (a consolation for Bombardier, for whom acceptance of the Montreal-Toronto electrification proposal would mean loss of an important LRC shop-window and erosion of the LRC's already tenuous hopes of export sales).

Unfortunately the state of Canada's national economy allowed little optimism that the Mulroney Government, however benevolent its smile on VIA, would act on the scheme. VIA are having to continue refurbishing old rolling stock, a program which should be completed by the end of 1991.

10
THE RAPID TRANSIT RAILWAY BOOM

The intercity train's struggle for purposeful survival since World War II has not been shared by the urban rapid transit train. The only significant battle in that sector has been for adequate funds to cope with the newborn anxiety of city after city to extend and improve systems, or in most cases to build new ones from scratch.

In the US, Washington first sensed the growing risks of downtown city sterilization by surrenders of more and more road space to the car, and the consequent need to inject fresh life into decaying public transportation, in 1961. That year's Housing and Urban Development Act included a modest emergency loan funding of financially-embarrassed railroads, directed chiefly toward their commuter services. That program soon proved to be hopelessly inadequate. The series of Acts which firmly grasped the problem with handsome provisions for Federal aid was launched under the Johnson Administration in 1964.

The starting point was the 1964 Urban Mass Transportation Act, a main aim of which was to enable public authority takeovers of ailing private transit systems. To that end it established a program of Federal matching grants, on the basis of two Federal dollars for each one put up locally, to help the preservation, improvement, and expansion of urban mass transit systems, subject to strict conditions concerning local planning; one objective under this head was to stimulate sensible integration of different modes of transport. The 1964 Act set up means of technical design and planning assistance for local operators, and also a Federal research and development program which was significantly augmented in amending legislation of 1966.

The 1964 Act set the stage for many of the regional transportation authorities which today oversee several different kinds of rail transport in some areas, as well as bus systems. Cases in point are the Metropolitan Transportation Authority of New York (MTA), which rules some 4,000 square miles focussed on New York City and oversees surface commuter lines once part of the various railroads submerged in Conrail, plus the Long Island Railroad and the New York Subway; and the Chicago Regional Transportation Authority (CRTA), which is sovereign of the Chicago Subway and of 463 route-miles over which five railroads run commuter services on its behalf under contract. CRTA itself, through its Northeast Illinois Railroad Corporation (NIRC) arm, runs some trains of its own, crewed by its own men.

The newborn operating bodies soon fastened on a shortcoming of the 1964 Act: its lack of assurance that Federal Assistance would go further than start-up money, because further aid funds were dependent on a year-by-year vote. That was put right in the Urban Mass Transportation Assistance Act of 1970, which massively raised funds set aside for the program to $10 billion and guaranteed continuing Federal support for at least 12 years, to the extent of $3.1 billion in each of the first five years. This legislation also created within the Department of Transportation the Urban Mass Transportation Administration (UMTA) to coordinate

Right: Baltimore, one of the newest US Metros, opened between Charles Center and Reisterstown Plaza in late 1983: Budd built the train-sets.

and manage the Federal aid programs. Three years later came a boost for rail elements of local development plans with a provision in the Federal Aid Highway Act of 1973 which allowed local authorities discretion to reassign Federal highway dollars to mass transit schemes. This enabled Boston, for example, to abort an expressway plan and claim some $1.4 billion for its mass transit program under the Interstate Transfer clause of the Act.

Federal subsidy of mass transit operating costs as well as of capital schemes was first established in 1974 legislation, which set aside $11.8 billion to meet needs under both heads up to 1980. The matching share of Federal grant toward a capital investment pro-

ject was now up from two-thirds to 80 percent; and running cost aid was possible for up to 50 percent of an authority's losses. The rising curve of Federal outlay on urban transportation reached its peak in the 1978 Surface Transportation Act, wherein President Carter signed away a total of $15.16 billion in UMTA capital grant and operating deficit aid for fiscal years 1979-83 (that legislation also included important "Buy American" clauses which stipulated, with only minor qualifications, that any contract worth more than $0.5 million must be placed with a US supplier).

Suspicion, so far as its rail applications were concerned, that some of the UMTA money was going not on hard-

Above left: Interior of New York Subway Type R62 car.

Below: Chicago Type 2400 train-set on downtown elevated section at Wells Street and Wacker Drive intersection.

Above: Berri-de-Montigny station on the Montreal metro.

Above right: A BART train hums away from Rockridge and heads east to Concord. In the background is San Francisco and the Bay Bridge.

Below right: Toronto Metro train heads south from Eglinton station.

nosed value buys but civic showpieces, and to perpetuate unrealistically cheap fares and outrageously featherbedded labor practices, was already worrying the Carter Administration in its final months. The new President Reagan, no believer anyway that a Midwest farmer's tax dollars should smooth a New Yorker's train ride to work, was sure UMTA money was misdirected. His determination to reduce capital assistance and cut out operating cost assistance altogether was baldly stated in his first Budget message: but of that and the outcome, more later.

The first North American city to build a new metro into its public transportation after World War II was Canada's Toronto, which opened its inaugural Yonge Street line at the end of March, 1954. Now a two-line system with 59 stations, almost entirely underground, this is comparatively tradition-

al in its third-rail, 570V DC current system for traction and in its train-sets, the first of which were built in Britain, the remainder in Canada. This is not so for the Montreal metro, begun in the spring of 1962, opening its first line in 1966 in preparation for the 1967 World Fair in the city, and now a four-line network that is still expanding.

Given Quebec's powerful French connection, it was unsurprising that Montreal should offer a North American bridgehead to France's rubber-tired metro technology. In this a train's carrying wheels ride on flat-headed concrete beams and their guidance is ensured by horizontally-mounted wheels on each flank of the truck which press against raised, lateral rails fixed at a constant gauge from each other outside the carrying beams or rails. The trucks also have orthodox flanged wheels for negotiation of switches. There the concrete beams are inclined downward, so that the train is lowered until its flanged wheels come into contact with the conventional steel rails in which the switches are laid and the rubber-tired wheels are idle. Beyond the switches the beams rise up again to accept the rubber-tired wheels.

The chief advantage of rubber-tired traction is its superior adhesion, which achieves a high rate of acceleration from stops, and the quietness of the ride which it imparts. There are debits: in particular, the excessive heat generated by the friction of rubber as the

tires bite into the beams in acceleration, which demands abnormally high-powered ventilation of the system at comparably high cost. Montreal metro riders suffered severely in the system's opening months, until the capacity of the initial ventilating plant was further increased.

If and when Montreal builds a fifth line, generally deemed essential to stimulate residential development east of the city, it is no foregone conclusion that this too will be rubber-tired. Outside its own metros, France has managed to implant its rubber-tired technology only in Mexico City and in some South American countries and there French industry seems to have a lock on all fresh equipment orders. So to realize Quebec's ambition of bigger world metro markets for its car-builders, notably Bombardier, a steel-wheel, steel-rail shop-window in Montreal may be deemed necessary, even

though that city's rubber-tired cars were all Canadian-built.

The financial traumas that almost incapacitated the first new US metro scheme after World War II added some stimulus to the initial UMTA legislation of 1964. The thought of carrying a rapid transit line under San Francisco Bay to integrate Oakland, San Francisco, and Berkeley, and thereby to forestall road traffic saturation of the Bay by bridges, had been floated as early as 1946. By 1957 the idea had solidified as a coordinated transportation plan for the whole Bay area, with the metro as its core, and an administering Bay Area Rapid Transit District Authority (BART) was founded to draft and execute the metro project. Four years later BART was ready with the outline of the most adventurously (for that time) and comprehensively automated rapid transit railway in the world.

BART's first crisis was financial. Litigation over bond-issue funding and rights of way stalled construction for two-and-a-half years, during which inflation made waste paper of original cost estimates. By 1966 BART was running some £150 million over budget. California's legislature eventually agreed to meet some of the excess expenditure, but the project was not totally secure until, in the nick of time, the funds were topped up by grants under the Federal two-thirds matching share clauses of the 1964 Act.

The civil engineering of the BART

Left: Automation nerve center: BART's all-network control room.

line was striking enough, with its centerpiece of a 3½-mile Trans-Bay tube enclosing two twin rail tunnels sunk to a depth of up to 135ft below water level. Astonishing, too, was BART's apparent determination to go for the unorthodox in almost all mechanical and traction engineering detail, from train-sets running on 5ft 6in gauge – deemed prudent for a smooth ride at the 80mph envisaged – to a third-rail current supply at the unusual value of 1,000kV.

The stunner, though, was BART's decision to go broke for automation, a leap into the unknown at the start of the 1960s, though the principles adopted were broadly those which govern today's metro automation systems. Issuing commands in the form of coded electronic impulses passed through the running rails, then picked up and decoded by apparatus on board the cars, one central computer complex would stop and start the trains, open and close

their doors at stations, and govern their speed between stops as required to match running to schedules stored in the computers' memory banks. When running got seriously adrift from schedules, the computers would automatically propose to the center's human controllers an optimal adjustment of train running to sort out the difficulty. BART was also the US pioneer of an automatic fare collection (AFC) system, of which more later in the chapter.

The 24-mile BART system opened in September 1972, but not until the early 1980s was it reasonably free of trouble. For the rest of the 1970s its creators paid heavily for reliance on such a phalanx of automated systems, many unproven in the rigors of daily metro operation – and, despite that, for building little or no provision for component failure into such vitally interacting systems.

Basic problems were, first, unre-

liability of elements in the automatic train control devices, including most importantly the track circuits. Other critical snags in BART's early years were train-set malfunctions and the fact that in certain conditions their programed rate of deceleration did not correspond with the signal spacing. This last flaw meant that if the trains were committed to the automatic driving part of the computer-based system, the automatic signaling and speed control element could not be trusted: to preserve spacing between trains, BART had to improvise a primitive form of human dispatching through interstation telephoning.

The vast amount of rectification and revision confronting BART enforced five-days-a-week operation only until late 1977. When seven-days-a-week working was finally attained in mid-1978, but at three-minute peak headways instead of the 1½-minutes originally anticipated, the ill-starred railroad suffered a major setback with an alarming train fire in the Trans-Bay tunnel, the consequences of which suspended all operation through it for 11 weeks.

BART's extensive revision of its control systems has now achieved reliability, and its trains log over 50 million passengers a year. Further proof of its value to the Bay Area is the commercial and residential development that has been spawned along its line of route. In 1984 BART was completely renewing its central train control computer at a cost of $27 million, to lift the number of trains moving simultaneously throughout its network from 49 to 75 (the original target had been 105), and beginning renewal of its car fleet with 150 vehicles from Alsthom of France.

These new vehicles would have what

Left: The smart interior of BART's Lake Merritt station.

Right: Washington DC transport integration: Metro train and bus against a backcloth of familiar US capital landmarks.

has become an almost indispensable feature of the electric rapid transit car – chopper control of traction motors, a most important application of electronics. The Thyristor (a form of transistor) obtains smooth, stepless acceleration as opposed to the old method of building up power mechanically, by progressively switching out resistances and varying the interconnection of traction motors. Chopper control is much more economical of current and additionally simplifies application of electrical braking, either of the dynamic kind or regenerative, in which the current generated by the reversed traction motors is returned to the supply rail or wire (but regenerative is only usable where there is immediate demand for the returned current – as in a rapid transit service, where nearby trains will be accelerating as others use their regenerative braking).

The first new metro scheme to take full advantage of UMTA capital aid was in Washington, DC. Construction of what was eventually to be a five-line, 101-mile network with 86 stations began in December 1969. By 1984 parts of four lines and almost half the finally intended route-mileage were operational, and over 300,000 passengers a day were using the trains. Capital costs had already passed the $5 billion mark.

The metro's operator, Washington Metropolitan Area Transit Authority (WMATA), was also harassed initially by glitches in the complex automation systems, though not so severely as BART's. The Washington network's computer-based automatic train control (ATC), soon perfected in operation, is typical of the labor-saving method applied to the working of a modern "full-metro" and so deserves description in a little detail.

The Washington ATC system is a product of General Railway Signal (GRS). It is an amalgam of three subsystems – automatic trains supervision (ATS); automatic trains operation (ATO); and automatic train protection (ATP). The link between these subsystems and the control of trains on the move is a sequence of electronic beacons (manufacturer GRS brands them as "Wee-Z" bonds) spaced at intervals between the running rails. Before departure on a journey, a transmitter on the train is preset by its single traveling crew member with its schedule number and destination in code. At its starting point and each subsequent station this individual train data is automatically picked up by the beacon and transmitted to the ATS computer, which compares the train's progress with its schedule and formulates appropriate instructions for dwell time at the station from which the data has been supplied, speed to be made to the next stop, and other performance requirements. These instructions are fed into the ATO system, which translates them into electronic commands to be passed to the train's receiver via the beacons.

The beacons also serve the ATP system. Track circuitry is registering the presence of trains section by section, and the spacing between them. The ATP compares this information with the commands set out by the ATO system and has fully overriding power to modify them if the state of track occupation or other factors prevent their safe execution as originated, no matter what the effect on punctual

working. It is the ATP-vetted version of the ATO commands which the beacons duly issue as coded electronic signals through the running rails, whence they are picked up by train-mounted receivers and translated into appropriate power and braking control adjustments.

Europe already has, in Lille, France, a totally automated metro on which trains are driverless, their doors opened and closed at stations under computer control as well as all other movement function, but WMATA is among the majority of the world's metro operators who as yet believe its trains should be minimally crewed, if only for the psychological reassurance of passengers. All that the single staff member of a Washington metro train has to do purposefully is to open and close doors, keep a watching brief on passenger activity, and broadcast station announcements over the train's public address.

Operations throughout the Washington network are monitored from one control center. Here operators face a dozen large color TV screens which show the entire track layout and automatically display the position and identity of each train, plus other vital information. The operators have a facility which enables them to call up on any of these screens a magnified representation of any section of the line on which they want to consider the traffic situation in more detail. They also have instant two-way radio communication with each train conductor and station staffs.

The Washington metro's inaugural train-sets, fully air-conditioned and capable of 75mph between stops, were US-built by Rohr, but that company has since exited the rail supply business. In 1983 WMATA began doubling its initial fleet of 298 cars with vehicles of similar but slightly modified detail design by Breda of Italy, which were shipped knocked-down for assembly in the US by Amtrak, in its Beech Grove, Chicago, shops.

Like BART, WMATA went for one of

Above left: Washington Metro's distinctive station styling: this is Crystal City.

Above: MARTA North/South line train in Atlanta shows the sensible way to travel to automobile commuters on Interstate 20.

the most elaborate forms of AFC, which was another source of teething trouble on both metros – so much so that in 1980 a top WMATA executive wanted to be rid of it in favor of something simpler, including a flat fare in place of WMATA's mileage-based and off-peak-variegated scales. The particularly vulnerable element of both BART and WMATA systems was the "stored-ride" facility, wherein automatic change-giving machines, which accept $1 and $5 notes, dispense magnetically encoded cards covering rides up to a total value of $20. At the platform entry the passenger slots his card into a barrier reader, which marks on it the originating station of the ride. At the destination the passenger inserts the card into an exit barrier, which automatically calculates distance traveled and deducts the appropriate cost from the card's value. If the passenger has over-traveled the value left on the card, the exit barrier will not open to him or her. An illuminated sign points to an Adfare machine, which for the necessary surcharge will re-encode the card so that the exit barrier will accept it.

The Washington metro was not short on distinctions. WMATA was, for example, the first authority in the US to integrate a thorough-going reorientation of its bus routes to serve as metro station feeders at the start of its metro network planning. It took care, too, to provide for suburban transfer from private cars to metro train for journeys to the city center; by 1984 its station parking lots had, in total, space for

some 30,000 cars. Its fully air-conditioned sub-surface stations were enormously impressive, both for their spaciousness and for their aesthetic style, which combined effective use of simple stonework with ingenious lighting.

There is little doubt that the costly grandeur of the Washington metro in particular was responsible for dampening the Carter Administration's enthusiasm for ever more generous UMTA capital aid, and for President Carter's own outburst against the "over-design" of some schemes. If the Democrats harbored such misgivings as they left office, a still icier view was to be expected from the incoming Republicans. Sure enough, in his first Budget message of 1981 to Congress, President Reagan sought to halve UMTA funding by 1986 and by then to have chopped UMTA operating aid down to nothing. Moreover, no UMTA aid would be forthcoming toward the capital costs of new metro building starts.

There was some justification for this douche, all political or economic philosophies aside. With the construction costs of a Washington-style full metro climbing beyond the $75 million-a-mile mark, some cities with aspirations to that sort of system needed a jolt to reconsider whether something less elaborate would meet their transportation demand adequately. An outstanding case of such worthwhile reappraisal was San Diego's rejection of a $1.2 billion full metro planned in the 1970s in favor of a surface light rail (LRT)

system that for most of the first line's 15-mile passage of the city's main suburban corridor could adapt an existing freight track, so that the capital bill for that first route was a mere $86 million.

The operating aid program, too, was ill-focussed. First, its formulae benefited the big cities which needed help least of all. Second, it lacked much stimulus to operational economy. Whatever their political allegiances, city politicos had been reluctant to keep transit fares in line with inflation, and few authorities had tackled labor costs, which in one or two cities were outrageously inflated by indulgent working practices and pay agreements with the unions.

In Boston, where the Massachusetts Bay Transit Authority (MBTA) ran out of money in December 1980 and had to shut down for 26 hours until the State legislature threw out a $41 million lifeline, employees were quoted as likening their featherbedded jobs to "dying and landing up in heaven." One factor was a short-sighted set of provisions in the first UMTA Act of 1964, intended to protect employees transferred from private transportation companies to the new public authorities, which at the same time handed the

unions a powerful voice in the affairs of an authority accepting Federal aid. An expert analyst calculated that transit workers' wages and benefits had risen by a staggering 400 percent in value between 1960 and 1980, or at twice the concurrent rate of inflation. After 1982, however, the cities were able to drive more realistic bargains on both pay and practices with the unions, partly thanks to the recession's effect on job prospects elsewhere. Even so, on average no more than 38 percent of operators' total costs was being covered by farebox dollars in 1984.

Up to 1984, Congress had frustrated the Reagan Administration's full retrenchment proposals. It had resisted reduction of UMTA operating aid below $875 million a year, compelling the Administration to put its elimination objective on the back burner until 1989; it had safeguarded total UMTA funding at levels rising from $3,650 million in 1983 to $4,150 million in 1986; and it had coaxed the Administration out of total opposition to UMTA capital aid for new metro starts, though in the spring of 1983 UMTA muted optimism on this count by honing its criteria for allocation of Highway Trust Fund money to new rail projects. More eagle-eyed scrutiny would be applied to such factors as cost-effectiveness, local financial commitment, local funding reliability, prospective ridership levels, operating costs, and transit time savings.

Highway Trust Fund dollars became available for transit in 1982, when one cent of a five-cent gas tax rise was earmarked for a new "Mass Transit Account." Imposed the following April, the increase was expected to yield $1.1 billion a year for transit purposes, which would be no more than a fraction of total need. But revived gas sales soon generated $1.5 billion a year and the Reagan Administration promptly went to battle to resist Congress pressure for handover of the excess $400,000 to the Mass Transit Account.

Assured availability of some ongoing UMTA funding at least cheered the Metropolitan Atlanta Rapid Transit Authority (MARTA), Maryland Mass Transit Administration (MMTA) of Baltimore, and Metro-Dade County Transportation Administration of Miami, all of which had embarked on full metros but were uncertain of ability to complete as planned; and also for the Southern Californian Rapid Transit District, aiming to end Los Angeles' now discredited monogamy with the car by construction of a metro from down-town via Wilshire Boulevard to North Hollywood. But the funding proposed through the mid-1980s would surely not run to full percentages of grant for all the dozen or so rapid transit construction starts, the majority of them light rail, already in or heading for the UMTA hopper in early 1984 as US cities grasped the social and environmental value of railed urban transportation. Moreover, the sum earmarked for Washington, DC, would curb that metro's network size to about 75 route-miles, not 101, and would likely rule out final extensions into the capital's black ghettos.

The first section of MARTA's planned system of two lines intersecting in downtown Atlanta's business district was opened in 1979 and in 1984 both routes were being extended in stages. Fresh Federal funding ensured a start in 1984 on the projection of the north-south line through the city's most affluent suburbs to Atlanta airport. The MARTA system employs the same ATO control of its whole metro operations as Washington.

French industry scored the initial sale of MARTA cars, which are of the aluminum-bodied pattern that was a speciality of the Franco-Belge company. But Franco-Belge went bankrupt (with disrupting effects on fulfilment of its big electric mu car orders for French Railways and RATP, the Paris urban transportation authority) and, though it was subsequently taken under the wing of another French concern, MARTA placed its follow-up order with the Japanese firms C Itoh and Hitachi. Some of these vehicles' traction equipment, however, is being supplied in the US by Garrett.

The first 8 miles of Baltimore's metro was commissioned in November 1983, after strenuous opposition from highway-oriented factions in the Maryland legislature had finally been overcome and 20 percent local funding secured to match an 80 percent UMTA grant. For its rolling stock Maryland sensibly got together with Metro-Dade to work out with Budd, the only US manufacturer still in the car-building business, a specification that would suit both Baltimore and Miami metros – and, hopefully, appeal as a standard off-the-shelf model to subsequent metro-building authorities. So these two metros' cars, operated in married pairs, are of identical pattern, with stainless steel bodies and microprocessor control of the traction equipment, which features Westinghouse choppers and regenerative braking.

The southern half of Metro-Dade's Metrorail in Miami opened for business in May 1984 and the whole of its first 21-mile line from Dadeland South through down-town to Hialeah in the northwest became operational in 1985. Subsequent projection to the Miami airport, Little Havana, and West Dade was on the planning file. The high water table in the region forced elevation of almost the whole route on a viaduct, but this compulsory renunciation of tunneling has turned out a blessing. It kept the capital cost of the initial section down to an average of some $50 million, half the norm incurred in Baltimore's metro construction.

Metrorail is an economy model in some other respects; automation is partial and fare collection is primarily through coin-operated turnstiles, working on the basis of a flat fare for any journey, with multi-ride fare-cards limited to issues for regular commuters, students, the disabled, and senior citizens.

An important adjunct of Metrorail is Metromover, Dade County's brand-name for a form of low-capacity transportation now attracting widespread urban interest as a means of virtually on-call transportation for short-distance movement. Generally known worldwide as a "Peoplemover," it employs wheeled cabins – maybe rubber-tired and guideway-controlled, as in Miami, or steel-wheeled on tracks, and electrically powered (by Linear motor in one version) – that have standing room only, are slow-moving and run at very close headways without staff under fully automated control. Miami's Metromover is a 1.9-mile line that

makes a complete circuit of the city's business district from Metrorail's busiest downtown station, Government Center. It is expected to distribute to their offices 80 percent of the 50,000 commuters passing though Government Center station daily.

It is by no means only the newborn metros that have made news this past decade or so. The dire problems besetting the New York Subway, the world's second biggest for network size, third in number of passengers moved annually (over 930 million), but first in car fleet size (almost 6,300, all Motored) by far, made newspaper copy worldwide in the early 1980s. That was when its major harassments of a high below-ground crime rate, a disreputable, graffiti-abused state, and a daunting backlog of renewal and improvement expenditure were compounded by flaws in the innovative air-suspension trucks of the 754 R-46 type cars bought in the 1970s. In the 1980-81 winter, with up to a quarter of the system's cars unusable at times, a weary executive was heard to sigh that "the only way at this point to fix things is to shut down the system for a week and call in a faith healer."

At the end of 1981 the Metropolitan Transportation Authority (MTA), the body created in 1967 to administer all public transport in New York City and its seven surrounding counties, authorized a five-year investment plan grossing no less than $6.5 billion for New York City Transit Authority (NYCTA), the Subway operator. This vast sum was to cover everything from an updated current system, signaling modernization and station improvements to desperately needed new car purchases.

The subsequent new car orders were the biggest ever placed in US rapid transit history. MTA was funding the whole investment from its own resources, through local bond issues and other financial devices, and since it was not asking for UMTA aid it was not constrained to "buy America." The bids it accepted roused furious controversy because they were softened by very generous loan financing from government agencies in the manufacturers' countries. Budd in particular howled "foul" and vainly sought Federal intervention to have a Canadian order voided as unfair competition. That went to a hungry Bombardier for a total of 825 R-62 cars; a further 325 R-62s were entrusted to Nissho-Iwi and Kawasaki of Japan; and the only slice of the action secured for US interests was 225 R-68 cars to be constructed by Westinghouse-Amrail in a joint venture with the Francorail consortium of France.

One of the recipients of the MTA's 1982-86 capital spending program – certainly not before time – was the Long Island Railroad (LIRR). A wholly-owned subsidiary of MTA, the LIRR claims to be the third oldest railroad in the world still operating under the name of its birth. Running more than 700 passenger trains a day over a system that stems from New York's Penn station and eventually fans out into nine branches, of which the furthest reaches Montauk, 117 miles from Penn, the LIRR earned enough re-

Right: The PATH stock of 290 cars was the first completely air-conditioned rapid transit fleet in the USA.

venue from its 80 million-plus passengers a year to qualify as a Class I Railroad: but in 1983 it sought voluntary demotion to Class II to avoid the documentation necessary to establish Class I status, since its freight was comparatively meager. The hub of LIRR operations is the famed, eight-platform Jamaica station, where its routes converge to yield a peak-hour train movement every half-minute or so.

The LIRR is part-electrified at 700V DC third-rail and the MTA's 1982-86 allocation to it of $1,058 million would provide for conversion of a further 28.3 route-miles and also supply of 174 new Budd-built type M-3 electric mu cars. For its inner suburban electric working in New York City, Nassau, and Suffolk counties, the LIRR has been deploying a fleet of over 750 Class M-1 emu cars. Most diesel-powered trains are push-pull, formed from one-time emu cars converted in the 1970s that are flanked by a locomotive at one end and at the other by a locomotive devitalized through removal of its traction equipment to serve purely as a control cab. In 1984 the LIRR launched progressive remanufacture in its own workshops of its diesel locomotive stud, which for line-haul work comprised 28 2,000hp GP38-2s and 23 1,500hp MP-15s, all from GM-EMD.

Another item on the LIRR agenda in 1984 was the construction of a big new car storage yard in Manhattan, the virtue of which would be to curtail train layovers in Penn station and thereby lift peak-hour operating capacity in that terminal by some 25 percent. However, a corollary of that project seemed to be indefinite pigeonholing of a grandiose, $1 billion-plus scheme to thrust a new bilevel tube over the bed of the East River between Long Island and Manhattan, with one level earmarked for a Subway route, the other for the LIRR, so that the latter's trains

could be diverted to a new terminal closer to New York's social and commercial heart than Penn station.

New York City is also served by the impressive New Jersey rapid transit line of the Port Authority Trans-Hudson Corporation (PATH), which has transformed the Hudson & Manhattan Railroad line it took over in 1962. In 1972 PATH created the first completely air-conditioned rapid transit car fleet in the US and since then it has created superb new terminals below Manhattan's twin World Trade Center towers and in a multi-modal Transportation Center at Journal Square, New Jersey.

An authority with a domain as large and transportation systems as varied as MTA's is perennially vulnerable to charges of unfairly discriminating investment of its funds. That has frequently been the lot of the Chicago Regional Transportation Authority (CRTA), vilified by outer-suburbanites for overspending their tax dollars on the inner-city services of the Chicago Transit Authority (CTA), which include the metro, and allegedly underfunding the CRTA-managed commuter rail operations to and from the outskirts.

Overseas sales of the TV series *Hill Street Blues* have made much of the world aware of the centerpiece of CTA's six-route, 95-mile metro network – Chicago's historic downtown elevated loop, the last sizeable "El" in the US, which figures in many stockfilm interludes of the show (despite the fact that the series' exterior scenes are apparently shot in Los Angeles!). The "El's" 85-years-old structure, with its unbelivably sharp curves, underwent a $103.5 million rehabilitation in 1984.

But Chicago has earned a much more

significant niche in urban transportation history through its integrated, multi-modal planning when it launched its first post-World War II metro extensions. That was the adoption of a median strip between the two thoroughfares of the new Kennedy Expressway for a surface projection of the Northwest line in the direction of O'Hare airport, and the allocation within that strip of ample space for stations with good road-rail interchange arrangements – bus bays, ample parking lots, and plenty of room for autos to put down or pick up rail travelers and drive away without hampering other road movement, the so-called "kiss-'n-ride" transfer. By the end of 1984 a further, 80 percent UMTA-funded extension of the Northwest line, again mostly threaded along the Expressway, had implanted the metro in the O'Hare airport terminal. The CTA was also engaged in a big new city-center tunneling exercise to reorganize two of its routes, and was working up plans for a new line from the Loop to the southwest suburbs and Midway airport.

In Boston the Massachusetts Bay Transportation Authority (MBTA) was in 1984 in the throes of a $2 billion improvement program, part UMTA-funded, part capitalized by Interstate Transfer moneys as outlined earlier, which principally affected two of the four metro lines. The biggest scheme involved dismantling of the elevated sections in a complete relocation of the city's Orange Line between downtown Boston and Forest Hills. Many of Boston's existing cars are Canadian-built, by what was at the time the passenger car element of Hawker-Siddeley Canada, now transferred to Can-Car; and it was Can-Car which in 1984 won the MBTA order for 56 new cars, to a UTDC (Canada) design, though final assembly would be in the Boston area.

Until Chicago opened up its metro service to O'Hare, the only US city with direct metro access to its airport was Cleveland, where the single route of the Greater Cleveland RTA runs 19 miles from the city center to the airport

structural, elaborate signaling and other trappings of a full metro. Simultaneously, a number of Continental European manufacturers, notably in Germany, were transmuting the trolley – or tramcar – into a high-performance, high passenger/tare weight-ratio vehicle, generally known as a Light Rail Vehicle (LRV). That turned LRT into an attractive, economical-to-run mass transit system with less passenger capacity, granted, than a full metro,

terminal. In this valuable integration of urban transit and air travel, North America has so far lagged behind Europe, where in 1984 half-a-dozen major airports already had rail systems firmly embedded in their terminal complexes and several more such schemes were planned or underway. The Cleveland metro was yet another importing foreign car design in the mid-1980s, in this case from Tokyo Car of Japan, but with final assembly to be executed in Cleveland by General Electric.

Cleveland has also bought abroad, from Breda of Italy, to renew the fleet of its Shaker Heights line, rehabilitation of which to modern standard of light rail transit (LRT) was finished in 1982. The evolution of LRT to its current high-performance characteristics has given urban rail transportation perhaps its biggest fillip of all.

The stimulus to this LRT development was the wartime devastation of many mainland European cities' trolleycar networks. When postwar reconstruction was possible, several city authorities sensibly decided not to replace the tracks in their historic mid-street paths, but wherever possible – which meant chiefly beyond downtown limits – to segregate them clear of other highway traffic. After that, as national economies revived, and capital was easier to come by, these cities could think of dipping the tracks below ground where it was impossible to carve out a new, dedicated course: that was, naturally, downtown.

In short, they ended up creating a modest railroad, but one without all the

Top: Italian-built LRV of Cleveland, from Breda.
Above: German-built LRVs by Duewag in Calgary Transit service, Canada.

Below: Duewag-built LRV of Canada's Edmonton Transit at the latter's Central station.

but one capable of an invaluable contribution to the transportation plans of cities daunted by the capital cost of starting a full metro from scratch in the late 20th century. San Diego's enormous saving in initial outlay has already been cited.

Buffalo, Dallas, Detroit, Los Angeles (in addition to its embryonic full metro), Pittsburgh, Sacramento, and San Jose in the US, and Calgary, Edmonton, and Vancouver in Canada have already either completed, embarked on, or are set to begin an LRT system. Denver should have been on the list, but in 1984 its Transportation Board was glumly reassessing the plan for a 77-mile LRT network in that region of Colorado following an unexpected voter thumbs-down for local sales tax funding of the project. The Dallas Area Rapid Transit (DART) scheme, aspiring to a much more ambitious 12-line, 160 route-mile network by early next century, did win electoral endorsement of sale-tax funding for its first phase, which envisages completion of as much as 69 route-miles (including an extension to Dallas-Fort Worth airport) by 1995.

The chief contestants for LRV orders are Japanese, Italian, and German firms. San Diego, for example, has bought the highly-regarded Frankfurt U2 model of the German company Duewag, a European major in the LRV art. (In Canada, Edmonton is operating a close kin of the U2, also Duewag-built.) European practice favors car articulation, not only to save weight and minimize energy consumption but also to simplify resort to sharp curvature of the track in tricky urban locations. Some European LRV types are three-car on four trucks (with the center car invariably ultra-short), but the U2 is two-car on three trucks. From the two of its three trucks that are powered, each with one motor, it gets a total output of 400hp for its 30.5 tons tare weight, a top speed of 50mph and can pack in 200 or even more passengers, 64 of them seated. The modern LRV has, moreover, all the electronic refinements of chopper traction motor control and dynamic or regenerative braking; in the Edmonton system, cars have a triple braking system – power-operated discs, electromagnetic rack brakes (beams mounted close to track level that exert retardation by subjecting the rails to magnetic force), and dynamic.

Canada's Vancouver is installing a mainly elevated LRT line employing a traction system which its progenitors, Urban Transportation Development Corporation (UTDC) of Toronto, has also been beavering away to market to US cities. Cynosure of its effort has been Detroit, where UTDC has already sold a Peoplemover system employing the same traction method.

This is the linear induction motor, which in effect reverses the two main elements of an orthodox electric induction motor. The linear motor has no rotor and consequently it does not impart power through a drive to the vehicle's carrying wheels, but by electromagnetism. The linear motor creates in its fixed stator an electromagnetic field which reacts with an aluminum and alloy plate, known as the reaction rail, laid between the running rails, to produce motive power; braking is obtained by reversing the motor's current. Another novel feature of UTDC's aluminum-bodied Vancouver cars is their patent steerable axles, which pivot on a yoke so that the wheels follow the running rails through curves and any squeal of wheel flanges is obviated. One attraction of the linear motor principle is that its elimination of most moving parts in the motor itself, and of gears and transmission drives, reduces maintenance.

Having commissioned its first 13½-mile line from the city center to New Westminster in 1986, the Vancouver LRT has the Seltrac system of automatic train control devised by the German company Standard Elektrik (SEL). This is a version of the method known as "moving block," in which, utilizing an inductive link between vehicle-mounted coils and cable loops laid in the track, computers on the vehicles and in the LRT control center continuously exchange data that is processed into commands to ensure safe spacing between following trains. In other words, the moving trains carry with them the means to establish, wherever they are, the block-section separation provided by a conventional trackside signal system and track circuitry. Seltrac automatically lengthens the distance between trains as their speed rises, so that space for braking increases with pace. But it allows Vancouver to run the LRVs in perfect security at headways as brief as a minute.

This chapter has not yet exhausted the areas of likely new rail development in the US. Houston has been excluded from the discussion so far only because at the end of 1987 its Harris County Metropolitan Transit Authority (METRO) was involuntarily reconsidering what kind of transit system to pursue. Back in 1982 the city had taken what seemed to be a rock-hard decision to start building a two-line, 75-mile full metro, even steeling itself to foot the whole construction bill if Reagan's Washington refused to countenance a 70-80 percent grant (at the time, as already mentioned, plans for new full-scale metros were anathema in the White House). UMTA funds were however, forthcoming, construction bids were called and preparations were taken as far as ordering 130 cars of Japanese design for 1986-87 delivery. But in June 1983 METRO was stunned by a decisive voter refusal to finance the scheme by a revenue bond issue. Only recently has the majority of public opinion changed in favor of METRO's plans.

Elsewhere, Milwaukee, Jacksonville, Orlando, Sacramento, and New Orleans were all reported to be weighing up urban rail schemes of one kind or another. The $64,000 question, as intimated earlier, is the extent to which budgeted UMTA funds for the rest of the 1980s will cope with fresh claimants for heavy support of capital expenditure.

INDEX

Figures in *italic* refer to illustrations in the text.